DR MUSHARRAF HUSSAIN
ADEEM YOUNIS

READ THIS BEFORE YOU MARRY

A Must Read For
Every Single Muslim

Read This Before You Marry
© 2024 Dr Musharraf Hussain and Adeem Younis
First published by Invitation Publishing 2024
www.invitationpublishing.co.uk

Cover Design and Typesetting by Convey
Printed and bound in Turkiye by IMAK OFSET
ISBN: 9781902248394

British Library Cataloguing in Publication Data
A catalogue record for this book is available from the British Library

The Forest Stewardship Council® is an international
non-governmental organisation that promotes environmentally
appropriate, socially beneficial, and economically viable
management of the world's forests. To learn more visit www.fsc.org

Authors' Introductions

Read This Before You Marry is a guide to marriage for Muslim men and women. It is a collaboration between Dr Musharraf Hussain OBE, DL, Al Azhari and Adeem Younis.

Dr Musharraf is a distinguished British Islamic scholar, educator and writer, the author of the Plain English translation of *The Majestic Quran,* published in 2018. In 2009, he was awarded an OBE for his services to community relations in Britain. He was also the Chair of the Christian Muslim Forum, a senior trustee of Muslim Hands and trustee of National Centre for Citizenship and Law. Formerly, he was the Director of Postgraduate Course in Education, and Vice-Chair of the Association of Muslim Schools. He is the author of many books, including *Time To Marry,* a guide to marriage for Muslims on which this popular version, aimed at a younger audience, is closely based.

Adeem Younis is a British entrepreneur and philanthropist. He founded the digital marriage platform, SingleMuslim.com, in Wakefield in 1998, and as a result has helped to facilitate over 250,000 Muslim marriages. In 2009, he founded Penny Appeal, a British charity working in 60 countries to provide essential aid and welfare to those in need. In 2021, he wrote and published his memoir, *Small Change, Big Difference: The Penny Appeal Story,* his bestselling account of his early life growing up in poverty in Wakefield and his determination to build both a globally successful business and a charity which since its foundation has reached over 49 million beneficiaries.

Dr Musharraf Hussain

All praise is for Allah, the Lord of the universe, the majestic creator, the sublime designer, the generous cherisher who gave humanity the gift of love and compassion so that they could live together as husband and wife. Blessings be upon the finest of Allah's creation, a source of kindness to the universe, the leader of the Prophets and the master of the believers, Muhammad ﷺ.

In a society where many are beginning to question the necessity of marriage, seeing it as outdated and irrelevant, the starting point is to discuss the reasons why the institution of marriage is still important. If you look at most media, relationships have become disposable. Celebrities who are role models for many young people seem to hop from one relationship to another – almost as many times as they change their outfits. So, with the way the world is going is there even a need for marriage?

Our Prophet ﷺ said that "Marriage is half the faith and complete your faith by developing *Taqwa*". What does that mean? What is the purpose of marriage? Many of us will have heard of the word *Taqwa*. We'll look at what it means and how it relates to marriage.

We are bombarded by different concepts of romance by the media which is clouding people's expectations and beliefs. The music we listen to is about falling in love... the books we read, the celebrity gossip we follow... all these condition us to have what is an unhealthy expectation of what relationships should be. 'Reality shows' and 'Soaps' abound on the TV. Everywhere we look the sanctity of marriage is being eroded and I know that a lot of our young people are being dragged into this, normalising what is effectively haram or strictly forbidden in Islam and in most other religions. They are beginning to question, 'what is the need for commitments like marriage?' Relationships like everything else have become about instant gratification.

So how does a young Muslim navigate relationships today with all these conflicting messages? At a time when secular forces are working hard to undermine this sacred human institution, it is even more important to remind young people about the sanctity of marriage and the role it plays in building and strengthening faith.

As the Blessed Prophet ﷺ said,
Marriage is half of the deen, then complete the other half by acquiring Taqwa. — Baihaqi: Reported by Anas

Hopefully after reading this guide, you will be better prepared for marriage, having made a considered choice for the right reasons and gained a better understanding of what to expect.

Dr Musharraf Hussain OBE, DL
Translator of The Majestic Quran

Adeem Younis

As-salamu Alaykum dear readers,

First off, I want to say thank you for joining me on the journey that we're going to take together through the ins and outs, ups and downs, of marriage in the twenty first century. Our dear teacher, the scholar Dr Musharraf, wrote his wonderfully insightful book *Time To Marry* back in 1994 and I'm grateful to him for allowing me to produce this updated version, *Read This Before You Marry*, here in 2024 under the SingleMuslim.com banner.

I'd like to let you into a little secret: I wish I'd had this book when I'd been setting out on my own path. Why? Let me tell you.

Back in the 1990s, I was a skinny little Yorkshire lad from Wakefield, always on the lookout for ways to help my mum. We were a single-parent family as my Dad passed away when I was just six years' old — my Mum worked her fingers to the bone to bring the family up. By the time I left school, I knew I wanted to do more to help my mum, but I couldn't see how best to do that.

It was about that time that Mum and plenty of the neighbourhood aunties began to drop heavy hints about the M word. Mum would leave a photo of one of my cousins in Pakistan on the mantelpiece. An aunty would tell me about the nice girl who lived with her family over the way in Bradford. I genuinely appreciated their concern but no, that wasn't for me. I wanted to choose my own bride, I wanted to find someone who shared my goals and my dreams. Yet how could a lad still in his teens and with just a penny in his pocket do that?

That was my lightbulb moment. I rented a room above the pizza shop where I worked and persuaded a mate of mine to start designing a website which I decided to call SingleMuslim.com. That's right: I know it sounds desperate but I decided to set up a business to find myself a wife!

Twenty five years and over 250,000 Muslim marriages later — that's how many marriages we've brought together at SingleMuslim.com — my pioneering ideas became the world's most trusted online Muslim marriage dating site and app and I'm the lucky Dad of four beautiful children.

So why do I wish I'd had Dr Musharraf's book with me back then? Well, when you read this new version of it, you'll discover that he doesn't just talk about how and why to get married as a Muslim, he also talks a lot about how to make your marriage work. And there are plenty of lessons in there that the younger version of me could have benefited from.

I like to think of this book as part of my own *deen*, my way of expressing my faith. It's a book for you: young souls just stepping onto life's stage, carving out careers, building friendships that will hopefully stay with you forever. You're not just our future, you're the pulsing heart of today's Muslim community here in the UK.

Think about this book as a mixture of traditional wisdom together with some up-to-date advice and a thorough grounding in the guidance of our faith. *Read This Before You Marry* is a labour of love from Dr Musharraf and me to you, to help you build a fortress of faith in your marriage to last you a lifetime.

I would like to thank personally the many people who have supported us in the publication of this book, but in particular I thank Mehmooda Duke MBE for her incisive interventions and for co-authoring with me the Marriage Navigator in Chapter Nine.

May all God's blessings fall upon your own marriage!

Adeem Younis
Founder of SingleMuslim.com

CONTENTS

CHAPTER 1

ARE YOU READY FOR MARRIAGE?

Marriage: is it a match made in heaven or a thing of the past? A lot of people are wondering if marriage is worth it these days. The number of people walking down the aisle is plummeting faster than a rollercoaster.

But before you say "I don't" to the idea of marriage, let's take a closer look. Are we missing out on something big here? Maybe there's a lot more than meets the eye to this marriage thing.

Back in the day, people had some interesting reasons for jumping into marriage. Let's go back in time, way back. Hundreds of years ago, people tied the knot for totally different reasons. It wasn't just about love and happiness. The wealthy saw marriage as a way to protect and grow their fortunes. The less fortunate were all about creating an army of mini-me's to help out with the family business. And let's not forget about respectability – getting married meant having some clout in the community, no matter how much cash you had in your purse.

Now, let's talk about what it means to be a Muslim and thinking about marriage. You might be surprised to know that Islam was on the marriage train from day one. Meanwhile, Christianity was slow to hop on board, waiting until the Middle Ages to catch up, and even then Christian leaders mainly saw marriage as a way of keeping folk in line. Islam dug deeper, giving clear guidance on marriage from the get-go. That's a pretty big deal. So, let's get exploring and uncover the real scoop on marriage in the Muslim world. There's so much for us to find out and learn.

Islam, *Taqwa*, and Marriage

Before we jump in, let's get one thing straight: *Taqwa* is the key to understanding it all. *Taqwa* comes from the awesome Arabic word *Waqa* which means "to guard yourself" — and not just against anything, but against anything that might displease Allah. Picture it as a way to cleanse yourself of all those evil traits and embrace the good stuff by steering clear of sin and embracing goodness. It's all about that inner state of mind, where believers are desperate to please the Lord. And how do they do it? Through devotion and selflessness, of course! It's like giving your mind a deep cleanse, getting rid of all those bad habits and filling it up with pure moral values. Sound like a challenge? Of course! But don't worry, every believer is up for the task. So buckle up: in the Islamic world, marriage and *Taqwa* go hand in hand.

Anyone who respects Allah's symbols, displays true piety of the heart. AL-HAJJ: 32

Successful is the one who meets Allah with a pure heart.
Al-Shura: 89

The Majestic Quran itself is a book of guidance which in its opening verse encourages us to observe *Taqwa:*

This is the Majestic book, there is no doubt in it, guidance for the pious. — Al-Baqarah: 2

The three characteristics of the pious are:
We who believe in the unseen, perform prayer and spend in charity from what We have provided them. — Al-Baqarah: 3

In the Quran, men and women are dubbed *Muhsin* and *Muhsinaat* — this comes from the Arabic root *Hisn* meaning a "fort". Basically, they're fortresses! You know what that means? It's like building the ultimate stronghold. When a man and a woman join forces in marriage, they become an unstoppable force. That's why marriage is such a big deal in Islam — it gives us the strength to resist temptation and stay focused on God. This is how you can become the real thing: a power couple.

But let's be clear here. God knew what He was doing when He created attraction between the sexes. And Islam doesn't shame us for that.

Instead, it celebrates the wonder of it all. You see, Islam recognises that we humans have our weak moments. So, marriage is like our secret weapon against those tempting distractions that could lead us astray. Marriage is the key to maintaining *Taqwa* — that deep sense of awareness, respect, and love for God. It gives us a solid foundation to build our lives together. So, why settle for anything less? Unite, be strong, and keep the fire burning!

The Muslim is inclined to believe that man has something more important to do than engage in a continuous battle with temptation, which he sees as a distraction from his principal business, Taqwa, which is the constant awareness of God. He thinks it's unlikely that men and women will resist temptation when it is offered.

— Hassan Gai Eaton

As Muslims, we all know that the Number One goal in life is to please the Almighty. And how do we do that? By embracing *Taqwa*. But wait, there's more. Islam has a genius solution to keep us focused on *Taqwa* and away from naughty temptations. It's called marriage. This holy union helps men and women resist distractions and stay on the righteous path. Don't just take our word for it, the beloved Messenger ﷺ himself said it:

Marriage is half of the deen, then complete the other half by acquiring Taqwa.

You see, marriage for Muslims isn't just about the two of you. It's way, way bigger than that. That's what makes this whole adventure so exciting!

But wait, what about romance?

Our lives are bursting at the seams with lovely dreams. Everywhere we turn, we're bombarded with gushy love stories. From Bollywood blockbusters to juicy novels, romance is everywhere. We've even got game shows pushing people to find their soulmates, and you can't take a stroll in the UK without being overwhelmed by products using romance to retail.

But hey, we can't deny that deep down, we all crave a little romance. And guess what? The Quran totally gets it. It knew from the start that we humans have our own needs:

Among His signs is He created spouses for you from your own kind, so you can live together peacefully; and He will put love and care in your hearts for each other, in that are signs for thinkers. Al-Rum: 21

Call it divine matchmaking, maybe. Allah had a brilliant idea to create a love story for the ages and it's called marriage. Forget about those fleeting flames that fizzle out like a bad reality TV show, we're talking about a love that lasts a lifetime. Two people, brought together by the ultimate power, bound by a sacred contract, and infused with all the love and compassion they need for a peaceful and harmonious life. This is a love story that honours not only their connection but also their devotion to Allah. Prepare to be swept off your feet by the magic of a heavenly bond between a man and a woman. As the Prophet ﷺ said:

Marriage is part of my Sunnah, and whoever does not follow my Sunnah has nothing to do with me. — IBN MAJAH

Tying the knot just because of some crazy romantic feelings? Not the best way to kickstart a marriage. It may sound romantic, but it's not the smartest move if you want a lasting relationship. Muslims know better than that. But here's the exciting part: love and romance actually grow and get better with time in marriage. It's like a little secret bonus of wedded bliss. So, why settle for a flimsy foundation when you can have love that only gets stronger year after year?

Let's talk about the perfect time for marriage

Maybe you're wondering, "When am I going to be ready for this whole marriage thing?" Well, there's an easy answer: the sooner the better!

Marriage in Islam is like a magical potion that brings strength and happiness to the lucky couple. So it only makes sense that the sooner you get hitched, the sooner you can start reaping those sweet, sweet benefits.

Islam is all about keeping it real and staying away from the crazy temptations of this modern world. And what better way to do that than by tying the knot early? It's like the ultimate antidote to today's one-hundred-mile-an-hour society. So, why wait? Dive into marital bliss and leave those pressures behind.

The blessed Messenger ﷺ himself encouraged youth to marry early: *Whoever amongst you can afford the expenses of marriage should marry, for it will lower the gaze and keep you chaste, and if you cannot afford it then fast, fasting is a shield.* — Nasai

The Prophet ﷺ didn't mess around when it came to preaching the benefits of marriage. Fasting is great for many faith believers, but Islam says marriage is where it's at. So, listen up: our wise teachers say, the earlier you say "I do," the happier you'll be.

The gift of marriage

Sexual relations within marriage are considered sacred in Islam. As the Messenger ﷺ said:

In every sexual act with your spouse there is reward for you. — Muslim

Now's the time to unleash your passion, desire, and yes, even lust! Allah recognises these as a natural part of being human. But here's the trick — as long as it's kept within the boundaries of marriage and treated with respect, it actually counts as an act of devotion. And by saying Allah's name before closing that bedroom door, you're taking part in an essential tradition established by the Prophet 鄴 himself. It's a reminder that these intimate moments between husband and wife are sacred. So, just as your love grows throughout your marriage, let your physical connection be another way to show your utmost reverence for Allah. It's both a pious and a pleasurable connection.

Maintaining modesty

Marriage isn't just about bringing joy to lovebirds — it also brings some major perks for both men and women. One of these sweet benefits is the promotion of *Haya*, the concept of modesty which is appropriate for all. Islamic teachings totally recommend it. Embrace the power of *Haya* and unlock a whole new level of awesomeness in your relationship, because the Messenger 鄴 also said:

When you do not have Haya you may do whatever you like. — BUKHARI

Every couple has the power within themselves to keep the sparks flying, but it takes a little effort. Don't let temptation creep in and disrespect the Lord. Enjoy the company of your spouse, but remember to steer clear of wandering eyes. Say no to all things crude, immodest, and shameless. By doing so, you'll not only keep the romance alive but also show your reverence for the Almighty. Keep the love burning and honour the Creator.

Jarir, a companion of the Prophet, asked: "Messenger, what should I do if I happen to cast a glance at a woman by chance?" The Messenger 鄴 told him to turn his eyes away. — Muslim

The first glance is excusable but the second is a major sin. The lowering of eyes enriches spirituality and enhances morality and that increases his love for the wife.

Islam is about submission to God's will. It's all about willingly obeying Allah's laws and showing total devotion. We're talking worship, *zikr*, charity, ethical conduct — the whole thing. And guess what? When we submit, we find peace with the Creator and our fellow humans. Talk about a win-win!

Now, let's talk fashion. For guys and girls, modesty is the name of the game. No showing off, no clinging clothes that leave nothing to the imagination. We've all got temptations, right? So, if you're flaunting your stuff, you're just asking for unwanted attention. We're all about keeping it classy and avoiding any unnecessary attention.

Marriage blossoms with *Haya* — it's all about showing even more devotion to Allah. So, embrace Islam, rock that modesty, and strengthen your devotion to the Lord. It's a winning combo for a fulfilled and spiritual life. Stay fabulous!

Marriage vs. Celibacy: Unleash your desires for a happier world

Forget suppressing your natural instincts, let's embrace them. While other religions try to hide their forbidden fruit, Islam takes a refreshingly different approach to our sexual desires. Allah created them for a reason, after all. So why not satisfy them?

Our very own Messenger ﷺ understood the importance of marriage in satisfying our appetite for pleasure. He even called it a form of worship, *ibadah*. Say goodbye to suppressed desires and say hello to a satisfying and fulfilling life. Join us in embracing our human nature and unleashing our desires for a peace-filled existence.

There are plenty of stories narrated in the Hadiths where the Messenger ﷺ wanted to see his companions married and living happily, with stable families. The Messenger ﷺ said:

Why do people make the lawful unlawful for themselves? Women, good food and sleep? Listen, I sleep, and I keep night vigils, I fast some days and not on others, I marry and whoever turns away from my Sunnah is not from us. — Tabari

By avoiding marriage and instead attempting to fulfil your religious obligations through celibacy...that's just going down a dead end. It is not what we were created to do and it's not what our Creator wanted us to do.

Marriage: The Secret Superpower

Are you willing to risk eternal punishment and the wrath of the Lord? Of course not! So why risk it by going against His will and engaging in sexual congress outside of marriage? It's explicitly outlawed, make no mistake about that.

While some Western thinkers have relaxed on the whole fornication thing, Islam understands that it's a crime against society as a whole. It's not just about the pain and damage to partners, it affects their children, families, and the entire community. It's like a domino effect that messes everything up.

Marriage, though, is here to save the day. Not only does it protect us from the dangers of fornication, it actively keeps society healthy. And why is marriage such a huge deal in the grand scheme of things? Because of family, the sweet cradle of love and compassion. Families are where boys and girls are born, grow up, and fulfill their roles in society. Marriage is like the heart and soul of a civilised community.

Let's embrace marriage as the pillar of the family and the cornerstone of society. It's not just good for us, it's good for everyone.

The Power of Kids: How They Shape Our World

We all know one thing: without kids, our species would be toast. Now, there's no question about it, raising healthy children takes some serious teamwork. That's why having a stable family life is crucial. Building a strong, healthy family is the key to raising amazing children. And marriage is still the ultimate foundation for that. By focusing on their well-being, parents pass down important values and traditions. It's all about helping each child reach their full potential and become a force for good.

We're all unique, and each of us has something awesome to bring to the table. So let's make sure future generations carry on that spirit. It's our job to keep bringing brilliant humans into the world.

But for Muslims, there's some extra spiritual incentive to marry and start a family. Seeking the pleasure of the Benevolent Creator is the name of the game. And here's how marriage can help: it ensures humanity's survival, brings more love to our beloved Prophet ﷺ, and even helps us score some blessings through the lives of our children after we're gone.

So let's celebrate the joy of children, because they're the game-changers who make our world brighter and better!

An eternal partnership filled with love

When two people say "I do," they're not just promising a lifetime of togetherness, but also a life filled with pure happiness, endless love, and a celebration of the divine. And all along the way, they're honouring the Greatness of the Lord. The Quran describes the relationship between a man and a woman beautifully:

They are like a garment for you, as you are for them. — AL-BAQARAH: 187

Get ready to say "I Do" because according to Allah, marriage is the ultimate connection between two people and it's a rock-solid commitment between the couple and Him. Allah expects us to go all-in and truly dedicate ourselves to this lifelong adventure. It's not just about being a good partner, but also recognising our responsibilities, duties, and loyalties to both our beloved spouse and the Creator.

Want to know more? Well stay here: there's plenty more of this good stuff coming your way.

CHAPTER 2

ARE YOU THE ONE?

OK, so you're in this room and there's plenty of people around and there's a lot of chat going on and someone's trying to talk to you about something but...it's no use.

You can't hear what they're saying. Because there's this person the other side of the room and it's like they've got a spotlight on them. You can't take your eyes off them. What's up? your friend asks. What? you reply. What did you say?

Boom! It's happened! Oh, you're in deep now, you know that? Your friend, she might as well be talking in Serbo-Croat for all you care. You haven't heard a word of what she's been saying. And you know why? That person the other side of the room with the cute eyes. That's why.

This is some serious stuff. Let's get the lowdown on just what's going on.

That lightbulb moment

What is it about someone that makes you think: the whole world seems different to me now? Sure, you're attracted. But what is it about them that's set those bells ringing? And why are you the only one that seems smitten?

There's all kinds of reasons why we might fall for someone. Let's check some of them out.

They look great. So, you think they're attractive, right? They're a looker. That's fair enough. We all love beautiful things. But what do you think is actually going on inside that brain of yours when you think: that's an attractive person? Take a look, you might be surprised.

Scientists tell us that there's no such thing as just liking someone's look. It's actually more about what those looks are telling us. That glint in the eye? It might make us think that person's really smart. The way he stands? Could be that you're working out that he's the sporty type, like you. The tone of her laugh? She sounds like a friendly person, maybe.

In other words, you can't just rely on that bombshell moment. You have to look further, find out what's going on behind those cute eyes.

You might have suddenly started feeling differently about someone because you keep bumping into them. First time: nothing. Second time: nothing. Third time: hold on a minute. Fourth time... it's called familiarity. That can trigger the lightbulb switch just as easily as those brooding dark eyes.

How about that person you often see in the queue while you're waiting for your coffee to be served? Last time, you noticed they had a book under their arm that you read last year. Co-incidence, or a meeting of minds?

Or you know what? That person the other side of the room: did you just log the funny badge they're wearing without really thinking about it? You like a joke, so that secret little voice inside of you is going, hey, we could have a laugh together.

What all this means is that there are lots and lots of coded signals, not all of which you understand when you find yourself so smitten. Which is why, even though this is a really exciting time, you need to take your foot off the accelerator!

Spoiled for choice

There's something else going on here, and that's connected with those clever little phones we keep in our pockets.

Back in the day, we just wouldn't see so many faces as we do now. We'd go to school, or go to work, we'd have our daily routines where we'd see the same people day after day. Familiarity, that's what it used to be all about.

But now, whether you swipe left or scroll through TikTok videos, you see more faces in one hour than you might have done in a week before! How can our overloaded brains keep up with all this information? Are we sure we really know why we like one thing or another about someone? Can we be sure we have a "type" when we're surrounded by so many foxy faces?

This is where it gets interesting. Faced with so much choice, we seem to need other ways of working out who's hot and who's not. And it may surprise you to know that what we often seem to do is seek out people who remind us of ourselves.

In case that sounds weird, it's not meant to be. You're not going to go through life looking for someone who's got exactly the same hair colour. But you are going to get interested when something about someone else makes you think: I think they think along the same lines as me.

In other words, you're starting to imagine spending time with that person.

Aha. Now we're getting somewhere.

This is where faith comes in

Do not marry an unbeliever until they believe. — Al-Baqarah: 221

The Quran always makes things crystal clear, and it's no different when it comes to marriage: the home should be a safe place of shared values. But you may find yourself drawn to someone who is not a Muslim. What then?

Do you think that person might be willing to become a Muslim? Will they be happy for your children to be brought up as Muslims? Do you dream of going on Hajj with your partner — well, will that work if they are not Muslim? There are all kinds of questions for you to think about and the best thing is to have open and honest conversations from the start.

These idoloters invite you to the Fire, whereas Allah, by His grace, invites you to Paradise and forgiveness. — Al-Baqarah: 221

Think about it. A person who lacks your faith may be more interested in things you can't relate to. Your marriage will be a long journey so just make sure you embark on it with someone who shares your values.

Have you seen him who made desire his god despite knowing otherwise? Allah let him go astray, sealed his hearing and heart and covered his eyes. Who will guide him now beside Allah? Don't you pay attention? — Al-Jathiya: 23

That's like the first decent hold on a climbing wall — now you're ready to aim for the top. You see, Allah is the wind beneath your wings when it comes to deciding on your life partner:

Don't despair of Allah's kindness. — YUSUF:87

Say: Keep doing good deeds! Allah and His Messenger sees what you do, so do the believers. — At-Tawbah: 105

A man or a woman filled with the faith is not just someone who speaks the Kalimah, they are filled with it from the top of their head to the tip of their toes. They understand their *Deen* and they practice it. So that is the wonderful news: Islam gives you some really cool tools to help you with your choice.

Moral women are for moral men, and moral men are for moral women. An-Nur: 26

Islam doesn't rate the glitz and the glamour of today's social media world. Money, status, influence...these have never driven good Muslims, not now, not for hundreds of years. No, what Allah has always wanted you to do is to be aware of faith. It's a different way of looking at people, it's about searching for that inner goodness in someone.

Find yourself thinking about someone's bank balance, career prospects, social influence? Well, just hold up a moment: those are material issues for much further down the line. Right now, you're looking for the spiritual values which can last you both a lifetime.

Whoever fears Allah, He will design a scheme for him to relieve his burden and provide and sustain him from a source he cannot imagine. — At-Talaq: 2-3

Sauban, who was a companion of the Prophet ﷺ, said this:

Each one of you should acquire a grateful heart, a remembering tongue and a believing wife who would help you in your affairs of the hereafter. — Ibn Majah

Now we're talking. A grateful heart, a remembering tongue, belief: these are the X-Factors for today's Muslims, nothing else. Points out of ten? You know how to mark your card now: is their heart and their mind illuminated with the light of Islam and the light of faith? Yes? Well you're off to a good start. The Prophet ﷺ himself said:

One who marries a woman for her honour, Allah will humiliate him, and whoever marries for her wealth Allah will make him a pauper and whoever marries for her noble descent Allah will make him lesser, and whoever marries a woman with the intention that she would lower his gaze and make him chaste or strengthen his relations, I pray Allah bless him and her. — Ibn Hibban

Can I marry someone who is not a Muslim?

Let's be clear about this: No Muslim can marry an atheist or an agnostic or someone who believes in multiple gods. So that means you can't marry someone who doesn't believe in God, you can't marry someone who questions the existence of God, and you can't marry a Hindu or a Buddhist.

Sounds strict maybe, but remember: marriage for Muslims is a spiritual union, it is something that Allah requires of us. Being married and being Muslim: they just go hand in hand.

Now, the Quran isn't strictly clear about whether men and women of our faith can marry a non-Muslim believer such as a Christian or a Jew. Most scholars today will tell you that it is believed the Quran permits a Muslim man to marry a Christian or Jewish woman, but does not allow a Muslim woman to marry similarly. Why? Because a Muslim man who marries a Christian woman is required by Allah to respect her faith and to encourage her to attend her own church. A Christian man marrying a Muslim woman, however, is not under such an obligation and so might make it difficult for her to practice her religion.

Want to talk through this more? It's a good idea to go to your mosque, chat with fellow believers, listen to your Imam.

Overall, most Muslim scholars will advise you: it is best for all Muslim men and women to marry other Muslims.

I'm ready! But where do I start?

You know what Allah wants you to do: He wants you to marry and He wants you to marry a Muslim. But maybe you're not super-sure now about whether you'll make the right choice for you — that attraction thing, it's complicated, remember?

Let's see where else you can turn for some rock-solid advice.

In the old days, families were the first people you turned to on this one. Your mum, your dad, your aunties and uncles, they all knew lots of other wider family members and friends, and they knew a bit about you too. So they were often the go-to people. And maybe today, it's not so different. Your mum knows more about you than you think! Your family might know about someone you haven't met who might surprise you — or they might have a view on that person you've secretly been dreaming about. No harm in hearing what they have to say. If you can't hear some straight talking from your family about that person you've been dreaming about, then are you 100% sure you know better than them?

But you might want to strike out on your own. Many more Muslims these days find their life partners themselves, without being guided by

Mum and Dad, so you're in good company. And there's plenty of ways to meet that special person. There are always lots of social and religious meetings and classes where you can chill out with people of your own age and faith. Try asking at the local mosque what events are taking place — you never know who might be doing the same thing! Same goes for sports and hobby meetings, where you've got a chance of meeting someone who loves football as much as you, or who can match your wicked chess skills.

Want to be a bit more determined about this whole matchmaking game? In your community, there will be some Rishta Aunties who make it their mission to sprinkle magic dust on two young people. They're not connected to your immediate family so you might feel a little more comfortable talking to them about who you've got in mind. There's plenty of wisdom behind those older eyes, so listen out for what they say.

And then, of course, there's the sponsor and author of this book! SingleMuslim.com has been helping young Muslims get together for a lifetime of happiness for well over twenty years. Now it brings together Muslims from all over the world and is the biggest and most accurate database you can find. Get clicking!

As Allah said:

People, We created you from a man and a woman and made you tribes and families so that you may recognise one another. The most honourable among you is the most pious. Surely Allah knows and is aware. — Al-Hujurat: 13

And the Quran mentions a divine promise:

Whoever fears Allah, He will design a scheme for him to relieve his burden and provide and sustain him from a source he cannot imagine.

AL-TALAQ: 2-3

CHAPTER 3

NOW YOU'RE ENGAGED

READ THIS BEFORE YOU MARRY

Way to go! You're engaged — big congratulations to you both.

It's an awesome step forwards, one that could shape the rest of your lives and give you free entry into the happiness club. You're still a long way away from the Big M, but you've made a really important step.

Wait though: what does being engaged really mean?

Time for *khitbah*

Muslims often call engagement *khitbah*, a little word which packs a lot of punch. *Khitbah* is a real contract between a man and a woman, so it's not something to take lightly. This is going to be the way you tell your families that you are serious about the possibility of a future together. It's a way of telling the world the same thing, a very public commitment, and what could be more exciting than that?

Most Muslim scholars tell us that *khitbah* is advocated by the Prophet ﷺ as a stage before marriage. Before the Prophet ﷺ was married to Hazrat Aisha and Hazrat Hafsah, he proposed *khitbah* to them first and announced the marriage. The Prophet ﷺ married Hazrat Aisha after an engagement period of three years.

Yes, *khitbah* is the real deal. When a woman becomes engaged she's called a *Makhthubah*, which means she is officially engaged. And that means that no-one else may propose to her while she remains engaged.

So let's celebrate! Let's get the families together, friends, members of the mosque perhaps, and let's tell the world. Exchange rings if you like (although remember: it is haram for a man to wear a ring made of gold — it's silver all the way for him). In Arabic, this exchange of rings is called *Dublah* and it's carried out with others at hand: you're not married yet so you shouldn't actually place the ring on your beloved's finger yourself, that's usually for another family member to help with.

Have fun at the celebration. This is your day, so do all you need to do to make it one to remember. This will be, inshallah, the only time in your life that you celebrate *khitbah* so come on, let's make it super special, but remember your Muslim rules: no alcohol or mixed dancing or forbidden foods. You want to start your life together as you mean to go on, and a fantastic *khitbah* celebration which accords with Islam's traditions is the way to go.

It's time to be sure

Now let's double-down for a moment on what *khitbah* means. It doesn't mean you're married — if that was the case, then you'd get married, wouldn't you? No, you've got engaged and what that means is that you've told your families publicly that you're thinking of spending the rest of your lives together.

Wow! That's some statement. Again, congratulations. But now you've worked out the difference, what should you be trying to get out of your engagement?

Well, what you really want to know now is: am I going to be happy spending the rest of my life with this person? This is your time to tell, so use it well. Once you're married, you're married for good, so while you're engaged, find out all you can.

Is the other person a happy person, for example? Do they seem like they're the kind of person who wakes up in the morning full of the joys of Spring? Do they like their job, their family, their home town? If you're not sure they do, then how can you be sure that when the two of you are actually together, they won't want to make some big changes?

While you're engaged, think to yourself: how did they react to this, to that? We all know that life can be stressful, that big challenges can come along at any time, so you want to be sure that the partner you've chosen is going to be up to those challenges, not crumple at the first sign. When you want a shoulder to cry on in the future, you want to know it's always going to be there.

If this all sounds a bit serious, then there's a reason for that: because it is! Your engagement is your one chance to find out if the person you love is also the person you can share the rest of your life with. So yes, celebrate and be happy; but also, take some time to sit back and examine the other person and examine yourself. Picture yourselves doing all kinds of things in the future, facing all kinds of challenges and ambitions. Are you sure you're both going to be sitting tight on that same page, walking hand in hand into every new day? This really is your time to make sure.

How to be together

You want time together during your engagement so you can find out more about each other. But you're still not married so don't forget a few do's and don't's along the way.

While you're still not married, you still shouldn't meet up together on your own. If you're true to your faith, you know that and you stick to that. Don't agree to meet up in private spaces, meet with family, with friends, with colleagues. You want to be able to spend time with your prospective husband or wife, so you can really get a sense of what they're like, but you don't want to lose your sense of modesty. Yes, find out whether or not the two of you click; no, don't flirt or play around with physical contact. Remember, you've got a whole life ahead of you and, until you're married, you both need to stay true to the rules of your faith.

Don't mistake being engaged for being married; instead, go about your *khitbah* with good intentions and you'll both profit from the time you spend getting to know each other. Allah wants you to make a success of your marriage, for all the reasons we talked about earlier, so He arranged for this time for you to be sure of your decision.

Muslim men and women do not gather in seclusion, or *khulwa*, with the opposite sex and that still applies while you're engaged. Make sure you follow Shariah law and have a chaperone-type guardian, or *mahram,* present when you meet up with your partner. You want the world to hope that you will make a happy marriage, so don't spoil that hope by jumping the gun.

Take the time to get to know their family. In Islam, marriage really involves two families for life so you need to ask yourself: will I be happy with his or her family? Because you'll be spending a lot of time with them once you are married! And also, even though people aren't always exactly like the rest of their family, you can tell a lot about someone by finding out where they came from. You meet their family and you really don't get on with them? Uh oh: what does that mean? Can you grow to like them, do you think, or are you getting bad vibes which might mean problems later on?

It's really up to you

Maybe the person you're engaged to came to you through a family introduction. That's been a route for centuries, so it's totally cool. But what if, during the time of your engagement, you decide this person is not the one?

You don't want to just ignore your family's suggestion because it came from them — like we said, your family often knows more about you than you think. But if you really don't feel like this is going to work, then Shariah law is totally clear: it's your right to say no. No-one can make you go ahead with a marriage if it's not what you want.

If this is your decision, then be respectful — to the person you're engaged to, your family, their family. If this isn't going to end up in a successful marriage, then don't make it worse by ending the engagement on a bad note. As a Muslim, you may believe that this marriage is not what Allah wants for you, and you may be right, so respect Allah too by being graceful and considerate in the way in which you end the engagement.

Remember: it's your decision in the end. You can't be forced into a marriage you're not sure about. So keep dignified throughout, you'll be pleased you were later.

There is a story that is well known about a courageous woman by the name of Khansa bint Khidam who came to the Messenger ﷺ. *She told him that she had two suitors: one was called Abu Lababa and the other was her cousin. She wanted to marry Abu Lababa, but her father had married her to her cousin, against her will. She pleaded: "Messenger my father has been unfair to me." The Messenger* ﷺ *replied: "this marriage is void, you may marry who you want." So, she married Abu Lababa* — Bukhari & Muslim

This just goes to show: all Muslim men and all Muslim women are free to marry according to their choice and it goes against Sharia law to force anyone to marry against their will. As we've seen, this doesn't mean that you shouldn't listen carefully to the advice of your family, your friends, your fellow Muslims at the mosque — but it really is in the end down to you.

Do I need to ask my mum and dad?

You've made your choice, you're engaged and you plan to go ahead and marry. Great! But wait: isn't there someone else you should be thinking about here?

That's right: Mum and Dad. Now, Muslim scholars don't all agree on whether you have to seek your parents' permission or whether you might do so out of respect to them. There's quite a difference between the two, as you can imagine.

Imam Abu Hanifa believes that parental approval is not necessary if you are marrying someone of the same social class or from amongst the family. However, his famous two students Imam Abu Yousuf and Imam Muhammad have a different take and see parental approval as a necessary condition for marriage.

And the Messenger ﷺ himself said this:
The marriage of a woman who married without the permission of her guardian is void, void, void. — Abu Dawud

There has always been this idea of getting the approval of someone senior in the family. It's the same for other religions too: the old Christian tradition of a man going to seek the permission of his bride-to-be's father. You can see how it might make sense, if you think about how important the family bond is in holding everyone together in good times and bad. Families are the bedrock of society so why rock the boat? Maybe think about it that way: you don't absolutely have to seek your loved one's family's permission, but why not start as you mean to go on?

Seek the guidance of Allah

Some Muslims feel that their choice of a marriage partner is something they should best leave to Allah. This is the approach Muslims call *Istikhara*:

To seek divine guidance (Istikhara) is a greater blessing for the children of Adam and not availing this is a misfortune.

Not sure how to go about practicing your Istikhara?

Follow these easy guidelines:

• Make *wudu.*

• Pray two *rakats (nafl)* at any time, and then recite the dua of *Istikhara:*

   - O Allah, I ask you to grant power through your knowledge, and I seek power through your ability, and I ask you of your great bounty, for you are able, and I am not able. You know and I do not know, and You are the Knower of the unseen.

- O Allah, if You know that this matter (here name your need) is good for me in my religion, my livelihood, and the outcome of my affair, then decree it for me and make it easy for me, then bless me with it.

- O Allah, if You know that this matter (here you name your need) is bad for my religion, my livelihood, and the outcome of my affair, then avert it from me and avert me from it. And ordain for me the good wherever it may be, then make me content with it.

- It's best to recite the dua before sleeping, though this isn't required.

- Like other duas, it's recommended that you face the Qibla.

- It's recommended you open the dua of *Istikhara* with praise of Allah and by sending blessing on the Prophet ﷺ, and to close in the same way.

Don't be in a hurry to find the answer to your *Istikhara*. Be patient! In time, you will find out what is best for you.

CHAPTER 4

PREPARING FOR THE BIG DAY

It's here! The big day has arrived! All that waiting, all that planning, did you think it might never actually happen? Well, it has.

And yes, this just might be the day you look back on in ten, twenty, fifty years even and say to yourself: that was the best day of my life.

So let's get busy with that to-do list. What do you need to think about to make sure your day is unbeatable? Let's kick off with a reminder of how the day is going to go.

The ceremony

First things first: who do we need to turn up on the day?

Well, the two of you to start with. That might help, mightn't it? Who else? Your parents or guardian too, they must be there. You'll probably have all the wider families and friends, but your parents or guardian are a must. The bride is usually represented in the contract negotiations by her *Wali*, her father who usually 'gives away' his daughter. The *Wali* gets the consent from the bride. He must always get it directly from her: the bride has to express her willingness to enter into the marriage. In the case that the father is deceased or there is some reason that he cannot fulfil the role, then another male guardian or relative can take on that role.

The wedding ceremony itself is often conducted by a pious Muslim or the local imam. There will also need to be two witnesses to the ceremony — they can be picked from amongst those who are present.

First comes the sermon. This is the chance for the imam to remind the bride and groom about their marital responsibilities. So listen up! The imam will most likely talk about how the bride and groom can acquire *Taqwa*, the fear of Allah almighty. Remember what we mentioned earlier in the book about *Taqwa?*

The Prophet ﷺ said, "Marriage is half the *deen*, complete the other half by acquiring *Taqwa*." [Mishkat]. So in the process of getting married, you're also establishing your Taqwa, which will support you in the years to come.

Here's how the Prophet ﷺ used to open the wedding sermon with Allah's praise and follow it by reciting the following Quranic verses:

Believers, fear Allah as He deserves to be feared, and do not die except in state of submission to Him. — Ale-Imran: 102

People be mindful of your Lord, He created you from a single person and created his partner from him, and then from the pair He spread countless men and women throughout the world. Be mindful of Allah in Whose name you make demands from each other and take care of the relatives. Allah watches over you. — An-Nisa 1

So, Allah may improve your deeds and forgive your sins. Anyone who obeys Allah and His Messenger has won a mighty victory. Al-Ahzab: 71

The ceremony itself ends with the prayer of the Prophet ﷺ:
May Allah bless you and may blessings be upon you and may your coming together be fruitful.

Getting down to details

The actual contract that the bride and groom agree during the ceremony is called the *Sighah*. Here's how it works:

Firstly, one of you makes an offer of marriage to the other. This is called the *Ijab*. The words which you use during the *Ijab* will be taken from the Arabic words used in *Ziwaja* (marriage) and *Nikah* (wedding).

If the other party agrees to that offer, this is called the *Qubul*. You can use any wording in the *Qubul* as long as it's clear that you have accepted.

The Ijab and the *Qubul* need to be carried out in one session in front of the two witnesses.

And that's all that is required. By adding anything else to the ceremony, any conditions of any kind, you will make the wedding invalid. So: keep it simple! Stick to the long-honoured Islamic practice and you'll be blessed.

The Nikah

Everyone's wedding day is going to be different. That's part of the beauty of it: it's your marriage, it's special and no-one else can ever create a day quite like it. But for Muslims, there is one unchangeable element, which is the *Nikah*, the actual Islamic ceremony of marriage.

The *Nikah* takes place when both of you say "Yes" at the ceremony. Both bride and groom need to say out loud that they consent, and put in writing that they consent. That's the *Ijab* and *Qubul* we just mentioned. Both of you need to be legally allowed to give consent, so you have to be old enough and not in any way mentally impaired. You need to know what you're doing here!

The *Nikah* then makes you married in the true Muslim sense, but you must remember: you also need to register the marriage formally within UK law. There are quite a few mosques in the UK which aren't officially approved under UK law to conduct marriage ceremonies, so if your *Nikah* is conducted in one of them, you need also to register the marriage in a recognised registry office. Don't be tempted to avoid this element: just in case something does go wrong inside your marriage, you will have no protection under UK law if you haven't officially registered the marriage in an approved centre.

The Mahr, or bridal gift

Islamic law legally requires that a Muslim husband must agree a financial payment to his wife. This is known as the *Mahr*.

Give women 'you wed' their due Mahr graciously. But if they waive some of it willingly, then you may enjoy it freely with a clear conscience. — AL-NISA: 4

The *Mahr* is often paid as money but, as long as the bride agrees, it can be paid as jewellery, home goods, furniture, a house or land. What's most important is for the bride and groom to agree on the amount and the form it takes before the ceremony so that you can both agree the exchange voluntarily during the marriage ceremony. No surprises makes for a happier day! Usually, to make sure there's no doubt or confusion, the terms of the *Mahr* are set out in the marriage contract which both parties sign.

According to the Sunnah, the value of the *Mahr* can be 400 dirhams of silver which was the *Mahr* of the daughters and wives of the Prophet ﷺ, but it can of course be any amount which the bride and groom and their families agree in advance.

Once the marriage has been consummated, the *Mahr* is the wife's property. Why's that? Because the *Mahr* establishes the bride's financial independence from her parents and gives her a real financial independence even, in some cases, from her husband. Once given, it remains hers for life.

There is in England a tradition of paying a Dower to the bride, but this is very different to the Islamic *Mahr*. The *Mahr* is a legal requirement under Islamic law whereas the Dower is voluntary, and also the *Mahr* is payable at the time of the marriage ceremony, whereas the Dower is only paid to the wife on the death of her husband. There's also some further confusion in some areas of the world where a dowry is given by a woman to her husband at the time of marriage, but this is not part of Islamic teaching.

There is one other story it is well worth mentioning connected to the *Mahr*. Al Nisaee, in his collection, reports a Hadith about Abu Talha. Abu

Talha proposed to marry Umme-Saleem. She said to him, you are an unbeliever, and it is not permissible for me to marry you, but if you embrace Islam then I will accept that as my *Mahr*, and I will not ask for anything more. Abu Talha agreed to become a Muslim and that was his gift to his wife. Sabit said, I have never heard of a woman with a more honourable *Mahr* than Umm-e-Saleem.

So just remember: the only safe way to ensure you conduct this element of your marriage ceremony according to Islamic law is to seek advice from your family and from your imam, and follow the the same path they suggest.

Further points: what about a prenup?

You've probably heard about prenuptial conditions, often shortened to "a prenup" in newspaper stories about famous people. It's basically a legally binding agreement drawn up before the marriage, often about the disposal of money in the event of the marriage breaking down.

Well, it's also acceptable for Muslims to set up prenuptial conditions if the bride and groom feel that it would be useful. For example, such an agreement might set out where the couple will live or whether either bride or groom will continue their education or career after marriage. Basically, any condition that is allowable under Islamic law can be made part of the marriage contract, provided that both parties agree.

What you can't include in any prenup is anything which would go against the essence of marriage: for example, saying that there will be no sexual intimacy between the two, or saying that one partner will not support the other during the marriage. A marriage is a sacred union in Islam and certain principles are not to be shaken.

To ring or not to ring?

The wedding ring has been part of marriage the world over and across all cultures. Back in the day, the ancient Romans and Egyptians swapped rings when they said "I do". There's something very symbolic about the beautiful roundness of the ring, it's almost as though it's an expression of eternity — like your marriage is going to last forever! And who's going to take against that? So go ahead, exchange rings if that's what you'd like to do, enjoy the process of choosing and giving. Just remember though: the concept of "wedding rings" isn't an Islamic one, so you're not obliged to do it if that's not what you both want. If you don't swap rings, you won't in any way weaken the vows of the ceremony.

Time to celebrate!

Let off those party poppers — you're getting married! Come on, if you can't be happy and if you can't celebrate on your wedding day, then when can you? It's a fantastic day for you both, it's a great day for your families, your friends, the wider community. Get into the party mode!

So let's start planning. The Sunnah says that weddings should be "widely publicised" and that everyone who is invited should enjoy themselves. Well, that shouldn't be too difficult, should it? But let's not go over the top here. Here's some good advice on how much to spend on your wedding day:

Let the wealthy man spend according to his wealth and let the one whose income is limited spend from what Allah has given him. Allah doesn't burden anyone except with what He has given him. Allah will soon make ease after hardship. — Al-Talaq: 7

In other words, don't go crazy with the costs. Being extravagant isn't a good way of marking your wedding day. In fact, your wedding celebration should also include a share for the poor and the needy as an expression of gratitude to the Almighty and realisation of His favour. The Blessed Messenger 🕌 was himself a model of simplicity: at his own wedding party, he gave goat meat.

But yes, let's not forget: we're celebrating here. So let's see some presents being given to the new couple. Why not show your love for them? Aisha narrates the Messenger ﷺ saying:

Give gifts to one another and you will love one another. — BUKHARI

You can wear whatever you like at your wedding and your guests are encouraged to dress up in order to celebrate with you. So absolutely, use your imaginations and enjoy the occasion. Remember though, that this is an Islamic ceremony so it's better to dress formally and modestly. Men and women should cover their legs and arms and women may be asked to wear a headscarf if the ceremony is taking place in a mosque.

It's also possible that if the *Nikah* takes place in a mosque, men and women may be segregated during the ceremony. If this happens, then the male representative of the bride, the *Wali*, can accept the *Nikah* and marriage contract on behalf of the bride. If the *Nikah* takes place outside of a mosque, at a venue or at home, then it's up to you and your family whether there is any segregation.

Music and singing

You probably won't have music at the *Nikah* because it is, after all, a religious event. That's especially true if the wedding is held at a mosque. But what about the wedding party? Can we use music to celebrate?

Well, most Islamic advisers point out that music and singing were not only allowed but were often encouraged in the past. Here's Aisha, the mother of believers, telling us what the Messenger ﷺ said:

Publicise the wedding, perform it in the mosque and play the tambourine. — Tirmidhi

Aisha also reported that when an Ansari man got married, the Messenger ﷺ asked whether there would be entertainment, since the Ansar are fond of entertainment.

You should have sent along someone who would sing. — Ibn Majah

And here's Amir bin Saad showing how music was played in marriage ceremonies during the days of the Prophet ﷺ:

I came upon Kurza bin Kaab and Abi Masood Ansari in a wedding where young maids were singing. I said you two are the disciples of the Prophet and have the honour of being Badri's and all this is being done in front of you? They said, sit down if you wish and enjoy it with us and if you don't, go away, since amusement is permitted for us on wedding days. — Nisaie

So yes, music and singing can be encouraged at the wedding party. The Sufis have always used music to spread the teachings of Islam around the world, they actually believe that religious music can bring us closer to God, so don't feel you shouldn't make some noise. Remember too the devotional singing, known as the *Qawwali*, which was practised all those years ago in India in the 6th century by the great Saint Khawaja Moinuddin Chisti. *Qawwalis* enriched the spirituality of listeners and helped them feel closer to God.

It's fine, there's plenty of evidence and tradition within Islam for making use of music and singing at a wedding party. Use both to make your day special for you and all your family and friends but make sure you choose wisely. Choose songs which are joyful and entertaining but stay within the realms of Islamic teachings and it goes without saying, food and drink choices should be halal, so enjoy the mocktails. Avoid suggestive music or dancing if you want to keep within Islamic principles and an Islamic wedding framework.

SingleMuslim.com ®

SingleMuslim.com founder Adeem Younis started his business above a kebab shop in Wakefield at the age of 17...because his mum was trying to choose him a wife! Wanting to make his own choice of bride, he created a website which has now enabled more than 250,000 marriages (and they're only the ones we've heard about).

We now have more than five million members on our platforms, spread around the world, and we want to share some of the beautiful couples opposite. You can see many, many more online, either on the website or on the app. It's safe, it's halal, it's designed for Muslims like you looking to find their life partner.

Success Stories

Sedki & Shayda

"I took the 9-hour journey from Texas to London and she came to pick me up. She tapped me and said my name. I looked up and having her hair up in pony tail wearing this smile from ear to ear, it was perfect!"

Sonia & Abid

"I never dreamed as a young girl marrying a guy who's a certain way, works a certain job or looks a certain way. Emotional intelligence has always been the key. I'd never come across the full package until I met Abid through SingleMuslim, he's perfect for me, my happiness says it all."

Ahmed & Celina

"My mum doesn't have an extended Muslim family, so you know I tried friends, I tried going to events, those didn't work out so well for me mostly because of my background. With SingleMuslim there was a wide range of people matched to my criteria."

The Majestic Quran

The Quran is the most powerful, life-changing book.

We believe you should not only read it but also experience it. The Majestic Quran's now world-renowned translation provides clarity to the point of understanding, fosters a deeper connection to Allah and transforms the reader's experience. It will move you, rejuvenate you and most of all, deeply stir your soul.

Key features of The Majestic Quran include:

Easy to understand and in today's simple English.

Made for the modern-day and contextualised into contemporary themes.

Beautifully designed and presented for an optimum reading experience.

Contains Arabic verses and English translation side by side.

It's time to experience the Quran, not just read it. Let the words truly transform you, as you feel the power and majesty of Allah's message. Join thousands of readers worldwide who have already been moved and rejuvenated by this clear and authoritative translation. Are you ready to let the Majestic Quran stir your soul?

Visit MajesticQuran.co.uk to order your copy

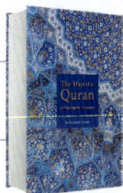

INVITATION PUBLISHING

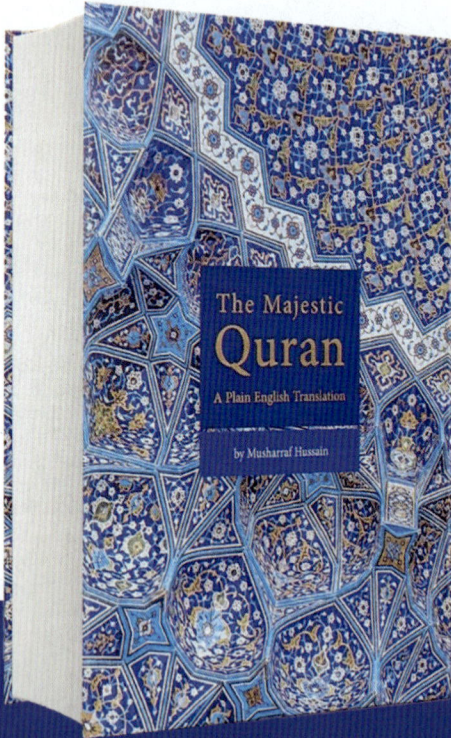

The Majestic
Quran
A Plain English Translation

by Musharraf Hussain

Experience the Quran like never before

CHAPTER 5

MAKING IT WORK

You wake up the next day as husband and wife. The sound of the prayers, the laughter, the happiness of the day before are still ringing in your ears. They'll ring in your ears for years to come, Insha Allah, the memory of that amazing day.

So what can you do to make sure that the two of you are happy in your marriage? Ever wondered how to keep love alive? It might sound a bit old-fashioned, especially with all those fairy-tale endings in movies and TV shows, but here's the thing: making your marriage awesome takes some effort. Just like mastering a video game or aceing a favourite sport, it's all about commitment. Your favourite TV characters might get their "happily ever after", but for us in the real world, it's about putting in the work to create our own fairy-tale ending. So, get ready to make your love story truly epic!

In many ways, it's all about justice and equality. Why? Well, think about it: justice is defined as "the practice of giving to others what is their due". You're not going to argue with that, are you? You give others their due, they give you what's yours. That's the recipe for happiness. There's something else though. The Quran teaches that men and women are equally able to realise their full humanity — they can both reach for the stars!

The believers, men and women, stand by each other; they enjoin what is good and forbid what is evil, they perform the prayer and pay Zakat, and they obey Allah and His Messenger. Allah will bless them, Allah is Almighty, Wise. He has prepared for the believing men and women, gardens under which rivers flow, they shall live here forever, in comfortable homes enclosed by gardens of everlasting bliss; and the Divine pleasure is the greatest reward of all, the supreme achievement. — Al-Tawbah: 71-72

There's equality too in the way the Quran uses such special language to affirm the equality of men and women inside of marriage:

They are your garment and you theirs. — Al-Baqarah: 187

Think about that for a moment. You always dress to make yourself look your best, don't you? You try and make an effort with your clothes, choose things which suit you. Well, a husband and wife, they fit each other like a carefully-selected set of clothes, and the beauty of those clothes gives us protection inside of our marriage because we are looking out for each other. As the Quran puts it so well:

Allah will put love and care in their hearts. — Al-Rum: 21

Marriage is like having a superpower — the incredible love between a man and a woman is one of the most amazing feelings ever. It's a special gift, given to them because they've chosen to follow their hearts and live in harmony with the universe. Allah weaves a magical bond between them, connecting their souls. In this bond, they find endless opportunities to be kind, to care deeply, and to make sacrifices for one another. It's a beautiful dance of love and devotion that makes their journey together truly extraordinary.

Marriage is just the best!

Men and women in marriage

In the Quran, it's crystal clear: men and women are absolutely equal, and fairness should guide our actions in every relationship. But equality doesn't mean being identical or like mirror images of each other — we're all amazingly unique. Being different doesn't challenge our equality; it celebrates our diversity. In our Muslim faith, we recognise that there are distinct roles within marriage. It's not about being the same, it's about respecting and embracing each other's differences, making our unions stronger and more vibrant.

The wife is the mother, the house builder, the bearer of children and their nurse and their teacher. Women give birth to children and have the innate ability to offer tender loving care to their offspring as a result of that intimate bond. Men, on the other hand, are on the whole physically stronger than women which is why the husband is the breadwinner, pays the bills and takes care of the family.

None of this is absolute or set in stone. Good men give excellent loving care to their children and strong women are able to compete in the man's world. So in today's world, we Muslims understand that our households are evolving and we are seeing more interchanging of roles within a marriage. There's nothing wrong with that, it just shows how flexible the Shariah is since equality is based on ability and preference rather than expectations and restrictions.

While we respect and adhere to the traditional gender roles of men and women in marriage, we know that the Shariah teaches us that men and women must be treated equally. Most Muslim countries have updated their family laws to suit changing times and nowadays, you'll find that Islam recommends a higher level of justice between men and women than most Western societies. Different but equal: that's our belief. Our gender differences are cherished Divine gifts to be adored, not to be used to keep anyone from being themselves. When a woman and man agree to get married, they agree to live according to the Shariah and therefore both are now bound to fulfil their pledge. We don't advocate the stereotyping of genders, but when a husband and wife agree to follow a traditional Islamic way of life then there should be no criticism of that.

Marriage is the sign of an incredible blessing, as Allah says in the Quran:

And from his signs is that he created for you a spouse from your own kind so you may have peace and comfort from each other, and Allah will put love and kindness in your hearts. There are signs for those who reflect. — Al-Rum: 21

It's for that reason — the chance that you have been offered to live a happy and fulfilled life — that it's worth putting the effort into making your marriage successful. Maybe we should take a look now at some of the rights and obligations that the Shariah sets down for us to make our marriage the success we want it to be.

By the way: these tips are very cool!

Tip #1: Love each other for the sake of Allah

Allah is the glue that holds a married couple together. When that glue sticks fast, it's known in the Quran as a *Mithaqun Ghaleesun*, or "a strong pledge". The pledge you make to your husband or your wife is one that you make of your own free will — we've explored already how nobody can force you into a marriage contract. So when you marry, you are sticking yourselves together and adhering the both of you to Allah.

When you agree to love someone else for all time, what you're really saying is that you're making your love for Allah the centre of your partnership. You love that person so much that you want the love to last forever, beyond this lifetime and into the Hereafter, where you can live in eternal happiness with them. When you love someone this much, you love them because they remind you of Allah and help you to get closer to Him.

Tip #2: Say Thank You!

The way you behave, your character, these are important things in the eyes of God. The Prophet ﷺ himself said:

There is nothing more important and weighty placed on the Scales than strong character. A person of strong character is like the person who fasts and prays regularly. — Tirmidhi

Each time that your husband or your wife helps you to be a better person, they are helping you to get closer to Allah. You feel like saying something mean about someone you know? You feel like they deserve it? Well, luckily your partner had the good sense to advise you not to, encouraged you to be a kinder person, and for that you should be truly grateful. So say thank you!

The Lord himself said just that:

If you are grateful, I will increase My favours for you; but if you are ungrateful, then My punishment is most severe. — Ibrahim: 7

Take the time to remember, then, that our spouses are a great blessing from Allah, because they keep reminding us of how we should behave towards others. Now isn't that just brilliant? Not only are you spending your life with someone you love and care for, but that person is also helping you every day to behave in a way that will please God.

That's definitely worth saying "thank you" for!

Tip #3: Keep Talking

One of the surefire signs that things aren't going so well is when you stop talking to each other. When things are going well, you tell each other everything: how your day went, the joke someone told you, what's on the news, what she thinks about this, what he thinks about that. Nattering to each other, that's such a good sign!

But sometimes it's easy to forget. We have busy lives, as the years go by routines can set in which somehow exclude the other person. What's most important is that you make an effort to recognise this, and then do something about it. Picture this: you and your partner, totally in sync, having a blast together, and still deeply in love even amidst all the chaos. How? Well, it starts with the little things. Sure, life gets hectic, but taking a few moments each day to remind your partner how much they mean to you can make a world of difference. Sit down with your husband or your wife, find out what is important for them to hear every day. Try and be the answer to the dua that Allah has taught us:

Those who pray, Our Lord give us happiness from our spouses and children and make us leaders of the pious. — Al-Furqan: 74

Some people say that men and women want different things, that men are more about the physical side of life and the respect that they get given, whereas women are more about the softer sides such as love and caring and discussion. Maybe there is some truth in that, as there is usually truth in many things, but also it's not absolute: men and women are equal in their humanity, Allah created both with a sense of human dignity, with physical desires and hearts that have feelings. The truth is that both men and women need love, respect, physical and emotional satisfaction, and they bloom like flowers in Spring when they get it.

So, what does it take to become a beautiful sight to look at? The starting point could be as simple as to smile at your spouse. You can always find a reason to smile at your spouse.

Smile because there's no reason not to. You should also make a real effort to look good for your spouse. If we accept that you will be the only man or woman your spouse is allowed to look at from head to toe, then don't let that be a sight for sore eyes!

What should a wife expect?

Yes, men and women are equal under Islam, but that doesn't mean they are the same or have the same needs. Both husband and wife should be able to expect certain things, to know for sure what's on offer. So let's start by taking a look at what women should find on the marriage menu.

Firstly, as we discussed in the last chapter, they must receive a *Mahr* from their husband. That is their absolute right and it forms part of the wedding contract. On top of that, if she plans to continue her education and training she should be permitted to do so. No ifs, no buts. Under Islam, a wife also has a right to enjoyment and entertainment. The Prophet ﷺ mentioned several times that the husband and wife should enjoy entertainment together, and encouraged married couples to keep up family ties and friendships. We'll read later on how family and friends can help married people when the kids arrive and one of the partners is working all hours, so dive in to that pool as soon as you can. It really can be a lifesaver.

A wife has the right to expect her husband to provide for her in a material way: food and clothing, a roof over her head. While the Shariah doesn't say that women can't take up a job to earn money, it does also say that it is the husband's responsibility. These days, with tough cost of living situations, many couples discover that they both need to work to make sure the bills are paid and that's completely fine too, if that's what you both agree.

Most Islamic scholars reckon that the husband should be responsible for providing all the furniture fitments and domestic appliances needed for a comfortable home. But it's important not to get too caught up in the pressure of having the best sofa in the street, the nicest car. Families can get into debt by trying to keep up with what they see in their neighbours' houses. We Muslims know there's more to life than flash appliances.

Once again, the Prophet ﷺ provides the best teaching on this. When he married his daughter Fatimah to Ali, he gave a simple *Jihaz* consisting of a leather bag for storing water, a pillow and mattress filled with palm leaves. The lack of material things and luxuries did not stop the couple from being happy together, in fact they were a perfect married couple.

Not all scholars agree one hundred per cent on the tradition that the husband should provide all the materials for the home. The Maliki Fiqh school of Islamic law suggests that the bride should use the money from her *Mahr* to contribute to the fitting out of the home. It's probably best to consult your family and your local imam on this.

What should a husband expect?

Islam sets out what a husband should expect just as it does for a wife. His wife should be loyal to him, should live alongside him and be pleasant to him. Here is an interesting view from the mother of believers, Aisha:

*Someone asked the Messenger who has the greatest right
on a woman?*
He replied, "Her husband."
I asked, "who has the greatest right on a man?"
"His mother" was the reply.

So with this example, the man has the final say in one instance, the woman in the other. Islam has skilfully avoided the trap of making one sex more powerful than the other. The two sexes are equal in the sight of their creator and the superior is the "one who is most pious". Whether you are a man or a woman, you are both equal in the eyes of Allah.

A woman who prays regularly, protects her chastity and obeys her husband's will enter paradise from any gate she likes. — MISHKAT

The successful wife stands by her husband when he needs her strength and support. Life is long and features both good times and bad — illness can arrive unexpectedly, financial problems can arise out of the blue. On these occasions, a strong wife supports her husband and gives him the encouragement he needs to get through the difficulties and out to the other side.

Here is another inspiring story from our Islamic faith: A bedouin complained to Amir Muawiya about the Governor of Madinah. The bedouin had a beautiful young wife, the Governor wanted to separate the bedouin from this wife so he could marry her himself. The two parties came before Amir Muawiya who said to the beautiful woman: "Which one of us do you like, the Amir ul Mu'mneen with his honour and palaces or the Governor with his anger or the bedouin with his hunger and torn clothes?"

The young woman pointed to her bedouin husband and sang an Arabic couplet:

Even if he is hungry and in tattered rags
He is dearer to me than my family and neighbour
Dearer to me than the one with the crown or Governance
Dearer than all the people with Dirhams and Dinars

Her loyalty to her husband and her intelligence amazed Amir Muawiya who ordered that compensation of 10,000 dirhams be paid to her.

The moral of the story? It's faith, love and loyalty which make a marriage shine like a diamond.

Living with the in-laws

If you get married to someone, are you going to be expected to move in with in-laws? Let's be quite clear: while in some countries in the world it is a cultural tradition to live with in-laws, it is not an Islamic rule —

there is no Islamic obligation on anyone to live with their in-laws once they are married.

Sometimes a young married couple will live with in-laws for a short time while they "find their feet" financially, and this can be a real lifesaver while the pennies are being counted. Sometimes, both husband and wife may decide jointly that they want to continue to live with in-laws, and that too is great, as long as it's what both parties want. Remember, as with so many things about Islam, it is about equality and respect and communication.

If a Muslim woman lives with her husband in his parents' house, there can be issues about privacy, particularly when it comes to there being non-*Mahram* in the house. For example, if the husband's brother also lives in the house, the Quran is quite clear that he is not *Mahram*, so the wife needs to have her own space to live within the house, separate to her brother-in-law. This is even more important when the wife wears the hijab.

Both husbands and wives have a duty to be respectful towards and look after their parents, but that doesn't mean they have to live with them once they are married. No one — not even the husband — should force a woman to cook, clean and do daily chores to please her in-laws.

The husband and wife need to have the conversation with each other whether this is a short or long-term arrangement and the earlier this chat takes place the better. Talk to each other about it during the engagement when you're getting to know each other better because if you find you don't agree, it could be a real deal-breaker.

Talk about everything!

We've already mentioned this, but it's so important we're giving it another go! From the very start, ideally before the marriage itself — in other words, during the engagement period — couples should talk about what they expect from their day-to-day life once they are married. Neither the husband nor the wife is going to take over the role of the other's parent, you're going to be a partnership from now on.

This is a new relationship, and it's based on equality. So make up a list like this and talk through it:

- Do you share chores or alternate?

- If one cooks does the other clean and vice versa?

- What's the deal with finances?

- Do you open a joint bank account?

- Where do the direct debits come out from?

- Who pays what?

There's no limit to what you can't discuss and sort out in advance. Do you both share the same views about how to bring up children and, if not, how are you going to come to a compromise? Are you sure you've discussed how much time each of you is going to be expected to spend with your in-laws? What do you both like to do at weekends? If one of you is a cinema fan and the other is an outdoorsy-type, then maybe you might want to agree in advance about sharing both activities in the future.

The more you talk, the better your future life will be!

An ideal marriage?

There are many good examples from our faith about how a man and woman can make a successful marriage. It's well worth taking a look at one or two of them now.

Baihaqi narrated an Arab wise man giving final advice to his daughter on her wedding night:

Daughter, if your mother was here she would be better suited to give you this advice, alas, there is no one but myself. Listen carefully to what I say, you are leaving the nest that you have outgrown, and you are going to a place you don't know. To a companion you are not in tune with, be pleasing to him and he will be your sky, giving you shade of compassion and shower of love, be a carpet for him and he will be your support, be a mother to him, he will be your slave, never abuse or insult him, never leave his bed for he will forget you. If he approaches you, go nearer to him, if he stays away, you stay away as well, take care of his nose, ears and eyes, he should not smell from you but perfume, hear from you but goodness and see in you, beauty. — Hadaya ul Murshadeen

A similar piece of advice is offered by a mother to her daughter. She says to her:

Take these golden gems from me daughter:

1. Be content and moderate.
2. Live by listening and co-operation.
3. Pay attention to what he sees and smells. He should see beauty in you and smell fragrance from you. Brighten your eyes with Kohl (surma)!
4. Take care of his meals and comfort at bedtime. The flame of hunger burns and spoiling of someone's sleep is repulsive.
5. Protect his property and wealth and look after him and his honour.
6. Don't spread his secrets.
7. Be the most agreeable to him and his companionship will be everlasting.
Remember dear! You can never achieve what you love until you sacrifice your own desires for him and your own pleasures for him. I swear by God, he will choose you. — Hadayatul Murshadeen

A Muslim woman is a good wife and the blessed Messenger ﷺ praised the work of a housewife. He regarded what she does in the home to be no less important than pilgrimage, charity, fighting in the battlefield, visiting the sick or attending congregational prayers. This is illustrated by a Hadith narrated by Asma, daughter of Yazeed. She says she went to see the Messenger ﷺ, he was sitting in the company of his disciples.

I said, O Messenger, I am a representative of women sent to you, Allah has sent you with the truth for both men and women, we believe it and follow it, and we the women, we are confined in our homes, we bear children, and you the men, have an advantage over us, you attend the congregations, visit the sick, attend funerals, fight in the battlefield and if a man goes for the pilgrimage or the Umrah we guard his wealth and property and we praise you for your righteousness and rear your children. Shall we not be included in these activities and their reward Messenger?

The Blessed Messenger ﷺ turned to his disciples and asked them:
Have you heard more beautiful speech from a woman about her religious affairs?

The Messenger ﷺ then turned to Asma and said to her:
Go back to the women and inform them that a good wife who is obedient and agreeable gets the reward of all that you mentioned.
Tabrani

Our Prophet ﷺ gave us direct examples of these ideals of marital relationships in his own personal life. There is no clearer prophetic saying about a husband's responsibility toward his wife than his response when asked:

Give her food when you take food, clothe her when you clothe yourself, do not revile her face, and do not beat her. — ABU DAUWD

It goes without saying that any kind of abusive behaviour towards women is forbidden and runs counter to all Islamic teachings.

Marriage for Muslims is an ideal state and if you both follow the guidance of your faith, you will be truly happy.

CHAPTER 6

SEX AND INTIMACY IN MARRIAGE

Many people find it difficult to talk out loud to someone else about sex.

That's not surprising, because it is such an intimate way in which a man and a woman express their love for each other. It's not just Muslims who find this kind of discussion uncomfortable — it's a natural instinct for most people to keep these feelings private. It's like an unspoken language of love, a realm where emotions run deep, and sharing those sentiments can feel vulnerable.

This shyness is made so much worse in today's world by the widespread availability of sexual and pornographic material. Explicit material isn't just tucked away in dubious backstreet shops any more, it's available all over the world on smartphones with just a few ill-advised clicks. There's no getting away from it: pornography and sexualised imagery are no good for anyone, and they should always be avoided. We get it, talking about these things isn't easy, and with smartphones putting all kinds of stuff in our faces, it can get overwhelming. Here's the deal: that online stuff? It's like a fantasy world, not real life.

But guess what? Islam, more than any other religion, gives us top advice on how to be intimate in marriage which stops us having to be either embarrassed or to seek solutions elsewhere which may be haram. Trust Islam to find a way to help us make life more joyful, not less!

How does our faith pull this amazing trick off? Let's dive in and take a look.

Let's get intimate

Right from the start, the Islamic faith tells us that both husband and wife should be willing and able to satisfy one another. A married couple can face difficulties if they don't face up to this need. Islam is such a practical and sensible religion, it understands the power of sexual passion but — and this is the amazing part of it — unlike other faiths it doesn't shy away from talking about it. Islam understands that both men and women have sexual urges and that if those urges aren't satisfied inside the marriage, the temptation to do wrong and seek pleasure elsewhere becomes greater.

Islam wants us to be intimate with our spouse. It's not like saying, well, that might be OK — it's laying down the law! Celibacy is discouraged, as we've read earlier in this book, and also extramarital sex is strictly forbidden for both husband and wife. So, the solution is obvious: married partners should give each other the pleasure which is due to them. Islam does not view sex as purely a means of having children, it recommends sex between husband and wife as a way of deepening the intimate love between them and of giving both of them the pleasure their bodies desire. You can go as far as saying that for a husband and wife to give each other pleasure in this way, they are simultaneously seeking the pleasure and closeness of Allah while keeping sin firmly locked out.

There is a story of the Prophet ﷺ seeing a woman he found attractive. He instantly returned home to his wife Saudah, who was busy making perfume in the company of some other women. She got up and went to see the Messenger ﷺ and they both retired to the bedroom.

He said of this:

If a man sees a woman who charms him, he should go to his wife, for she has the same means of satisfying him as the other woman has.
Darimi

First night nerves

You are both going to be nervous on the first night. That's completely natural, this is a whole new world opening up to you. And because you'd like the rest of your married life to be happy and mutually satisfying, it's worth taking it slow.

Remember, Islam doesn't set out too many rules on intimacy, beyond encouraging couples to enjoy it. So be kind to one another, and don't expect everything to be perfect from the get go! You will have months and years to learn to know each other, and to find out from each other what you both like, so don't raise that bar too high on night number one.

Take it easy. Don't either of you try and force anything in the early days, just let time and your growing intimacy do the work for you.

Marriage to an older woman

There is a perfect illustration of the Islamic approach to the intimacy which a husband and wife can enjoy in the Hadith of Jabir.

Jabir was the son of a famous warrior from the Ansar tribe and had accepted Islam as a young boy, probably when he was only seventeen. His marriage took place shortly after his father was martyred in the Battle of Uhud.

Jabir reported that he was once on an expedition with the Prophet ﷺ and, when they got close to the city of Madinah, Jabir started to speed up on his horse. The Prophet ﷺ seemed surprised and asked him why he was in such a hurry to return home.

Jabir replied, "I recently got married!"
The Prophet then asked, "Was it to a widow or a virgin?"
Jabir replied, "A widow."
The Prophet said, "But why didn't you marry a younger girl, so that you could play with her, and she could play with you, and you could make her laugh, and she could make you laugh?"
Jabir said, "Messenger of Allah! My father died a martyr, leaving behind daughters, so I did not wish to marry a young girl like them, but rather an older one who could take care of them and look after them."
The Prophet commended him saying, "You have made the correct choice."
— Nasai

Let's take a deeper look at this Hadith of Jabir and work out what it is teaching us. Like so many of our teachings, it reveals some brilliant truths by painting a beautiful picture.

In the first instance, notice the frankness of the Prophet's ﷺ question. He is encouraging Jabir to find a playful wife and wants both of them to enjoy each other. This clearly shows that it is one of the primary goals of a marriage that each party find satisfaction in the other. Clearly, the words 'playfulness' and 'laughter' indicate that what is being encouraged is the couple's romance and their physical satisfaction with each other. Not only that, the Prophet ﷺ urges them towards 'having fun' with one other. Isn't it refreshing to read the Prophet's ﷺ openness with Jabir, especially when we consider how these days, some Muslim communities will shy away from even discussing love and romance!

Then let's look at the final phrase of the Hadith of Jabir which says:

So, when we were about to enter the city, the Prophet said to me, 'Slow down, and enter at night, so that she who has not combed may comb her hair, and she who has not shaved may shave her private area.' — Bukhari

Here we see that the Prophet ﷺ did not want Jabir to surprise his wife. At a time when there were no modern means of informing the family when a traveller would return, a crier would be sent into the city, announcing that the caravan was returning. So, what the Prophet ﷺ is telling Jabir is to wait for this crier before proceeding into the city. What these lines like 'combing the hair' tell us is that spouses should physically beautify themselves for one another. The Prophet ﷺ was telling Jabir not to be impatient and that it might be better for him to delay his arrival so that his wife could prepare herself for him.

The explicit command to shave pubic hair is an astonishing expression to find in a Hadith! We all know that a part of our Islamic tradition is that one must shave pubic hair – but notice how in this Hadith, the command is put in the context of the sexual act. In other words, the husband is told to be patient so that his wife may beautify her private area to increase the aesthetic pleasure and gratification of sex.

The lesson is clear: a husband and wife should take care of these things to please one another.

Togetherness

Islam understands human nature so well and wants to use that understanding to help us make of our marriage a happy union. There are many examples in the Hadiths showing us the way towards enjoying each other physically inside of a marriage, and there is nothing to be embarrassed or ashamed about in this. Imagine having a relationship where you not only love and support each other but also enjoy a deep, meaningful connection on every level, including physically. Islam shows us how to achieve this, making sure that both partners are happy and content in their relationship. It's a beautiful and positive approach that can make your marriage truly special!

We should, in other words, aim to have passionate sex lives in our marriage. And that means taking care that your loved one enjoys themselves as much as you. For example, Islam emphasises the importance of foreplay before sexual intercourse takes place: it is selfish of one partner to seek satisfaction when the other partner does not achieve it. It is often easier for men to achieve satisfaction than it is for women, which is why men are encouraged to arouse their wives before having sex.

The Prophet ﷺ himself discouraged sexual intercourse without foreplay: *It is lawful for you to go in unto your wives during the night preceding the (day's) fast: they are as a garment for you, and you are a garment for them. God is aware that you would have deprived yourselves of this right, and so He has turned unto you in His kindness and removed this hardship from you. Now, then, you may lie with them skin to skin, and avail yourselves to that which God has ordained for you.* — Al-Baqarah: 187

Do you see the delicacy of the wording? A garment brings satisfaction, comfort and warmth, so here men are being advised to give these to their wives during intimacy. The Prophet ﷺ also said,

Every game a person plays is futile except for archery, training one's horse and playing with one's wife. — NASAI

By this, once more, we clearly see the importance attached to mutual sensual pleasure. In another Hadith he said, *If any of you has intercourse with his wife let him be true to her. If he attains his pleasure before her then he shouldn't hurry her away until she also attains her pleasure.*

Couldn't be clearer, could it! A man who doesn't attend to his wife's physical needs is letting her down, and is also showing a lack of understanding of the true nature of what Islam entails in practice.

A few things to remember

While Islam is so wise about the needs of men and women, and how they may in their marriage express their love for one another and for God, it is also helpfully clear about what is not acceptable.

We know that having extramarital sex is forbidden for men and for women. What is also not acceptable is either having sex while the wife is menstruating or engaging in anal sex. Both are considered sins. A husband and wife may be intimate while she is menstruating, but they must not have intercourse until her period is over.

In Ramadan, when you are fasting, sexual activity is only permitted at night. And if you are undertaking Umrah or Hajj, it is forbidden to have sex throughout.

It's also important to remember that sexual activity means that a person becomes *junub*, which means unclean. If you ejaculate, or if you have intercourse even if you don't ejaculate, you must always take a bath afterwards. You may not pray until you have done so.

Don't talk to others about your intimacy. It's between a husband and a wife, it's not something for others to know about.

Oral sex is another intimate activity which can cause people to blush! But once more, Islam is wise and thoughtful on the matter and does not consider it to be haram, as long as neither partner takes bodily fluids into the mouth. Some scholars have suggested over time that this practice should be discouraged but there is no clear ruling against it in the Shariah. Suggestions that it is indecent tend to be cultural, so bear in mind the possibility that your husband or wife may not be comfortable. Once again, it's about achieving an intimacy which you both enjoy.

The Quran is silent on the issue of masturbation. Many scholars have expressed the view that it should not be practiced but others have suggested it is acceptable in certain situations, such as when a man or woman is for some reason on their own for a lengthy period. Once more, the most honourable solution is to aim for sexual happiness between man and wife and to communicate with each other at all times.

On the subject of planning when you have children, despite the fact that there are some Islamic scholars who oppose it, there is no specific Islamic rule against using contraceptive methods to delay the arrival of a family. It is understood that money issues or the health of the mother-to-be could provide a good reason for delaying having children, either through the coitus-interruptus or Al-Azl method of withdrawing the penis before ejaculation, or by contraceptive methods such as condoms or sheaths. Islam, however, does not in any way condone sterilisation, because this goes against one of the main reasons for marriage, which is to have children.

Scholars have unanimously agreed that abortion is prohibited when the foetus has reached 120 days. Some scholars insist that abortion should not be allowed if the foetus is less than 120 days. Overall, it is down to the individual couple to make their decision on this, as there is no clear Islamic ruling on it, but look at it this way: contraception is allowed by Islam as a temporary solution until the couple is ready to have children, but it cannot be used throughout a marriage, as marriage should result in children; abortion should therefore not be required unless in extreme medical circumstances. Remember this:

Those who kill their children foolishly without knowledge, and who forbid what Allah has provided them, falsely attributing it to Allah, they have already lost: they have gone astray; they aren't guided.
Al-Anam: 140

Keep talking

We covered a lot in this chapter, perhaps more than you've had to consider before, so hopefully it's been helpful.

Overall, a happy intimacy in marriage will emerge if both the husband and the wife can approach the subject with confidence. This may take time: young newlyweds will often lack experience at the start. But with patience and a caring approach, you can both stop feeling either shy or self-conscious and learn to enjoy what your faith encourages you to practice.

Once again, keep talking to each other. Don't blame one another for something you don't like happening when you are together, instead talk about it and explain to your partner how you would like things to improve. Be kind, be gentle, be understanding.

Use your own imaginations and your own growing intimacy with one another to keep the flame of desire alive during your marriage. Don't ever resort to those artificial sexual imageries which are so prevalent in today's internet. Learn to rely on one another, to trust one another, and you will have a blessed union.

CHAPTER 7

DISCUSSING DIVORCE

We don't really want to talk about divorce in a book about the blessed happiness of marriage, but our aim is to provide a practical guide to a happy union and it wouldn't be right to avoid talking about when things get tricky.

Life isn't always smooth sailing, but there are ways to navigate stormy seas and strengthen your bond, steering clear of the need for divorce. So let's explore how things can turn pear-shaped and explore ways in which it might be possible to change things for the better between the two of you and so avoid the need for divorce.

First off: Islam does not say you cannot divorce. When a couple really can't live together, and they've tried all kinds of ways to make it work, then Muslims are allowed to end the contract. But bearing in mind that marriage is recommended for all Muslims in order to bring more children into the world, to spread happiness and to express the glory of God, then divorce really has to be a last resort. The Prophet ﷺ himself considered it to be "the most repugnant of permissible things" [Bai Haqi].

The Quran tells us that marriage is a special kind of contract, stronger than other social contracts like leases, mortgages, political agreements and so on. Marriage is at the heart of human nature, it's a natural union that is rooted in the needs and desires of men and women. Marriage comes out of the love of a woman for a man and their mutual wish for unity, peace and a life of faith.

The Shariah wants us to build the relationship, to practice love and togetherness, not let that powerful bond slip. The Quran encourages us to step away from divorce if we can and to make the marriage work.

So before we look at how you go about getting a divorce, let's take a good look at some ideas on how not to have to do it!

I want my spouse to change

It's an old story, isn't it? I love my husband/wife, but I just wish they would...

Whenever anyone thinks or says that, what they actually mean is that they want their spouse to change in a way to suit them — they think in doing so, this will mean the marriage works better. But isn't that a bit self-centred? Isn't that like saying, I know what the perfect spouse should be, you don't! Behave like I want you to behave, and we'll be all good!

The Prophet ﷺ was always very clear on this. He said: *If there is a defect in your partner look for something good in him/her.*

And the Quran too: *Sometimes, you may dislike something that is good for you, and sometimes you may like something that is bad for you.* — Al-Baqarah: 216

We all need to remember that living with a husband or a wife is very different from living as a single person.

Both parties need to learn to compromise, which doesn't necessarily mean they need to change, but they need to be more tolerant and aware of their spouse's needs and desires.

You can go a long way towards solving those things that you find irritating in your spouse by looking at it in this way: both of you need to change in some ways to make the marriage work, don't try and make out it's got nothing to do with you!

I feel lonely

Life after marriage can throw some unexpected curveballs your way. Imagine going from the hustle and bustle of your family home, where noise was a constant companion since childhood, to a new place where it's just you and your partner — now and then, the quiet can be deafening. Or perhaps you used to spend your days working, surrounded by coworkers and the buzz of activity, but now you find yourself alone for hours while your spouse is away at work.

These changes might feel daunting, but they're also a chance to embark on a thrilling adventure together. Embracing the chilled atmosphere of your new space can open the door to intimate conversations and shared hobbies. Those solitary hours at home? They could become an opportunity to explore your passions, pick up new skills, or even start a creative project. So, while the transition might seem a bit overwhelming, it's also a gateway to discovering new facets of yourself and your relationship, making this journey all the more exciting!

Then, when your first little bundle of joy arrives, it can bring immense happiness but also a heightened sense of isolation. Balancing the demands of a new baby, household chores, and the necessity for one of you to work outside the home can make the days feel long and overwhelming. The constant hustle and bustle of parenting, coupled with the absence of your partner during the day, might leave you feeling a bit adrift. But fear not, this challenging phase is also an incredible opportunity for growth. It's a chance for both of you to strengthen your teamwork, support one another, and discover the amazing journey of parenthood together. With patience, communication, and a sprinkle of humour, you'll not only navigate these hectic days but also create beautiful memories amidst the chaos. Remember, you're not alone — many young parents are experiencing the same whirlwind of emotions and challenges. So, embrace the adventure, celebrate the small victories, and lean on each other; you'll emerge from this period stronger and more connected than ever before.

This is also where your community comes in. Overseas, in Muslim countries, this kind of isolation is very rare, because the society is very open, with friends and family in and out of each other's houses. In Britain, sometimes you have to work harder to encourage that sense of community, but it's worth it. You'll make new friends, and you'll be amongst people like you who are fresh on the road of marriage and trying to work it all out just like you are.

Once more, the best solution to feeling lonely when you're married? Talk. Talk to one another about it, and work out some solutions that will make you both happy.

I need more money

Did you know that money problems are the number one cause of divorces in the UK? So how do you avoid joining that statistic? How can we go about dealing with money problems in a marriage?

Firstly, talk to each other about your attitudes to money, ideally before you get married. Is one of you a spender and the other a saver? If so, can you both compromise a little and reach a middle ground? Can you plan to both save and spend so that neither of you will end up feeling worried or depressed?

But now you are married, new money problems might come up, so be prepared again to compromise if you need to. Neither of you should be miserly if there is money there. This doesn't mean you should be extravagant, and it certainly doesn't mean that you should spend money in order to impress the neighbours. But as the Hadith says:

A dinar spent in freeing a slave, a dinar spent on a poor and a dinar spent on your wife, the greatest reward is for that spent on the wife. — MUSLIM

Our UK society is overwhelmed with advertising and social media messages encouraging us to spend money on this and on that, and brands pay a lot of money to clever marketing agencies to convince us we need to buy things that, in all honesty, we probably don't. Talk about those marketing messages with your spouse, and try and focus on what your family needs in order to be happy, not what brand managers think you need in order to take your money!

I need more loving!

Marriage in Islam provides the lawful and cherished channel for fulfilling sexual desires. It's the sacred bond that unites two individuals and serves as the foundation for a fulfilling intimate relationship. When one spouse feels unfulfilled in this aspect, it's crucial to address the issue promptly.

Open and honest communication is key. Rather than succumbing to negative thoughts or seeking satisfaction elsewhere, talk to your partner. Marriage is designed to strengthen the connection between two people, not drive them apart. If you ever feel neglected or unsatisfied, don't hesitate to share your feelings with your spouse. Together, you can find solutions, reignite the spark, and foster a deeper, more meaningful intimacy. Remember, a strong marriage is built on trust, understanding, and the willingness to work together through challenges.

It's essential to consider that there might be underlying reasons if your spouse seems less active or interested in the physical aspect of your marriage. There could be personal or emotional issues affecting their desire, and without open communication, understanding these concerns becomes impossible. By talking openly and empathetically with your partner, you create a safe space for them to share their feelings and concerns. Together, you can address any issues, find solutions, and work towards rebuilding the intimacy in your relationship. Genuine and compassionate communication is the key to overcoming challenges and strengthening your bond as a couple.

Remember: being with someone else is not all about getting as much sex as possible. That's a corroding myth put out in permissive Western advertising, film and TV — it's just not true that we are all seeking to have sex as much as we can. What is true is that we want to have sex with our husband or our wife. No-one can tell you how much sex is the right amount, and our faith certainly doesn't try and instruct us on that. No, the only people who can tell that are the husband and wife, so you need to speak openly if you feel like you are unsatisfied.

You'll be amazed by what you can achieve by being open about this, as you will be about most things in your marriage.

I'm being badly treated

No-one likes to argue. We all want a peaceful life but sometimes we can end up arguing, bickering, picking quarrels with our spouse for no apparent reason. Sometimes this bad behaviour is the result of stress elsewhere in the marriage: money worries, health worries, fears about the future. Sometimes, unfortunately, it can result from ill will on the part of either husband or wife.

So what's the best thing to do if you feel you are being badly treated by your spouse, and you've tried to sort it out with them but nothing's changed?

The Shariah is alert to this possible situation and recommends a team of two mediators, one chosen by the wife's family, one by the husband's. The mediators can be family members or not.

The Quran says:

And if you fear a breach between the two, then choose an arbitrator from his people and an arbitrator from her people. If they both desire reconciliation, Allah shall effectuate concord among them.
Al-Nisa: 35

In the mediation process, it's like having experienced guides by your side. Picture this: you and your partner come together, and these mediators, instead of being stern, are like understanding friends. They ask questions, encouraging both of you to share your feelings openly. It's a safe space where you can talk about what's bothering you. But here's the cool part: these mediators don't just point out problems; they remind you of the awesome responsibilities that come with being in a committed relationship. They help you see past the issues and focus on forgiveness, understanding, and being there for each other. It's all about teamwork, and they gently nudge you towards solutions that work for both of you.

Think of them as relationship superheroes, guiding you away from the pitfalls of separation. They remind you how important it is to stay together, not just for yourselves but also for any little ones you might have. So, in a nutshell, these mediators are here to help you navigate the rocky waters of love, ensuring your relationship sails smoothly into the future. How cool is that?

All marriages have their ups and downs. Don't think that you're the only married couple who argue — it's much more common than you think! But most people learn how to avoid arguing, how to be kinder to their partners, how to be patient and have forgiveness. Surely that's a better way to go about things than just throwing in the towel?

That's why it's always a good idea to try and reach out to family members for help before taking this final step. You may not want to, but it's worth it, in case someone is actually able to help the two of you patch up your problems. Really, try every avenue before you say it's over.

The last resort

Well, you've both tried as hard as you can, but it's no good: you can't fix the problems in your marriage. If that really is the case, then don't beat yourself up about it — sometimes, we just can't get what we want. The Quran says:

The parties should either hold together on equitable terms or separate with kindness. — Al-Baqarah: 229

If you have both honestly done all you can to make your marriage work, and it still doesn't, then neither of you is obliged to remain in a situation that causes you distress, pain and suffering. Allah will permit your divorce if it really is in both your interests to separate, but He will still oblige you to conduct yourself with kindness and consideration. Above all else, you must think of the wellbeing of any children involved, and also consider the impact upon the wider family. Marriage is one of the most important binding elements of family and if you decide to divorce, you can't pretend that this won't have an impact on your parents, your brothers and sisters, your wider family.

We don't want to spend too much time on this last resort, divorce. This is a guidebook to help you achieve a happy marriage, and we would like all Muslim men and women to succeed in their marriages. But for the sake of completeness, we must finish this last section with one or two practical details.

When a divorce is initiated by a husband, it is known as *talaq. Talaq ar Raji* is what is known as a "revocable divorce" which means that, after the husband has made his pronouncement, it is still possible for the couple to resolve their difficulties and return to each other. *Talaq al-bain* is an "irrevocable divorce" and this means that the couple will go their separate ways and should never meet each other alone again in the future. If a husband initiates the divorce, his wife is entitled to retain her *Mahr*.

A wife can initiate a divorce in two ways: either by mutual agreement with her husband, which is known as *Khula*, or by going to the court and asking for an annulment, known as *faskh*. In this second case, she must demonstrate to her imam that her husband either did not look after her properly, or was insane or cruel, or inflicted violence upon her, contracted a contagious disease, became impotent, or simply disappeared. In all of these cases, the imam is likely to suggest that the wife should keep her *Mahr* after the divorce.

The husband, after divorce, will remain responsible for the financial support of his children. It is usual that the mother looks after younger children following a divorce, while older children can choose which separating partner they would prefer to live with.

A last word of advice

We tried to make this last chapter more upbeat than down, because in our faith we do believe that with kindness and generosity and empathy, we can make most things better. Marriage is no different. Your lifetime union with your husband or your wife is the solid foundation for your happiness and the happiness of those around you, so let's do our best to be winners!

CHAPTER 8

MAY ALLAH PUT BLESSINGS UPON YOU

On that unforgettable day when you stand tall and proclaim, "I do," you're not just starting a journey — you're beginning an amazing adventure!

As a Muslim, you're fulfilling the wishes of the Prophet ﷺ himself; as part of the community, you're stepping up to the mark; as a human being, you're diving headfirst into what could be the most incredibly fulfilling experience of your lifetime.

This guide isn't just a set of instructions; it's a roadmap crafted for young souls like you, brimming with excitement about sharing their lives with someone special. In the vibrant tapestry of Islam, we celebrate unity among generations. Here, the young draw wisdom from the old, and the elderly find inspiration in the accomplishments of the youth. It's a harmonious faith that urges us to share, listen, talk, and most importantly, to be kind.

Within these pages, we've done all we can to help you and your beloved embark on this beautiful journey, drawing from the wisdom of our faith and the shared experiences of youthful hearts entwined in love. Take your time, seek wise counsel, and above all, do what feels right for both of you. We're not just wishing for your happiness; we're cheering you on as you step into a joyous life together.

May your days be filled with endless laughter, unwavering love, and moments that take your breath away. Here's to both of you, embarking on this incredible adventure. May Allah shower you with success, robust health, boundless happiness, unyielding patience, and the strength to overcome any hurdle that comes your way. Good luck, and may your journey be blessed with love everlasting.

And as you set forth on this sacred path together, remember, marriage is not just a union of two souls: it's a bond woven with threads of trust, respect and faith. It's a commitment to stand together through life's joys and challenges, to uplift and support each other in times of need, and to cherish the beauty of togetherness.

As you navigate the ebb and flow of life, may your hearts remain steadfast, anchored by the values you hold dear. Embrace the differences that make each of you unique, for it is in celebrating these differences that you'll find strength and resilience as a couple. Let the love between you be a guiding light, illuminating even the darkest of days, and let that love form part of your own *taqwa*. Communicate openly, nurture your friendship, and let kindness be the language that echoes through your home. Remember to express gratitude for the blessings bestowed upon you, and may your love story inspire others to seek the beauty of companionship grounded in faith and love.

Your marriage is a testament to hope, a testament to the enduring power of love in a world often fraught with uncertainties. So, hold onto each other's hands with unwavering trust, for together, you have the power to create a haven of love and tranquility that stands as a beacon of hope for generations to come.

Congratulations on this beautiful journey together, and may the love you share continue to blossom and flourish for eternity.

People, be mindful of your Lord, He created you from a single person and created his partner from him, and then from the pair He spread countless men and women throughout the world. Be mindful of Allah in Whose name you make demands from each other, and take care of the relatives. Allah watches over you. — Al-Nisa: 1

CHAPTER 9

THE MARRIAGE NAVIGATOR

READ THIS BEFORE YOU MARRY

We have provided you with a navigator, relevant to each chapter, designed to help you travel through the journey of marriage in a smooth way.

We hope that it will give you a helping hand when you feel a bit stuck and nudge you over some bumps in the road. The navigator is designed to give you food for thought as you make one of your most important life decisions, choosing the person that you plan to spend your life with.

It is worth remembering that one of the best marriage navigators is probably that set out in the Sunnah of the Prophet ﷺ. What did he do? At the age of 25, he married an older woman, a successful businesswoman who was also his boss. He had a beautiful monogamous marriage with her until she died. He then entered polygamy but only after his first wife's death.

He married women of different ages and cultural backgrounds. There is an abundance of guidance within the Sunnah which is always worth considering if you get stuck.

Meanwhile read on for some practical suggestions to help you to navigate this exciting journey.

Chapter One: Are You Ready For Marriage?

Will you ever feel ready for marriage? We have spoken to many young people who say that they were not looking to be married until they finished university, or after they were established in their career but then they met or were introduced to someone who they only agreed to see to keep the family happy and Cupid struck. So, you may never feel ready as such. Here are some things to think about when you meet or are being introduced to someone. Ask yourself these questions:

- What have I got to lose if I agree to meet someone that my family or friends are trying to hook me up with?

- When you meet them, was the conversation effortless or did you struggle to find things to chat about?

- If you like them, ask yourself, what do I have to lose from getting to know them in an official Islamic way as opposed to doing things the un-Islamic way and dating them?

- Imagine the beauty of getting to know someone in an Islamic way, in Nikah and the blessings that come from this?

- What do I have to lose by getting married early?

- What do I gain from marrying early?

Here are some things to think about:

- Having fun together in a halal way and being free to be together.

- Having the blessings of the family as opposed to trying to date in secret!

- Security that you have a loving partnership and friendship which is halal.

- Being there to support and nurture each other through Uni or your early careers.

- Growing as two individuals together.

- Having the blessings of Allah.

Chapter Two: Are You The One?

Decisions, Decisions, Decisions! How do you decide if this is the person that you want to go on life's journey with?

You are probably wondering, how on earth will I ever know if someone is the right person for me? Is it about physical attraction or are there deeper more meaningful things that I should be thinking about?

These questions may help you to navigate the challenges that we face in knowing if we have met the right person and looking beyond the superficial.

Remember that you are making a choice for life, possibly in your late teens or at some stage in your twenties.

Some questions you may want to think about and may find helpful to consider.

- What are your 'deal breakers?' or what is your 'Ick?' What matters to you so much that if your partner has or doesn't have these qualities you cannot see yourself proceeding with the marriage. If you don't know what your deal breakers are, the questions below may come in handy.

- Work out your negotiables. Where are you willing to compromise? How much are you willing to give or change your views without feeling resentful?

- What are your core values? What really matters to you in life? What drives you?

- Write down at least three things for each question. These may help you to understand yourself a little bit. If you understand yourself, you will have a better chance of being able to work out what you are looking for in a partner.

- What are your future partner's core values? Do your values align? Are you both driven by similar things? Does this matter to you? Talk about this with your potential partner.

- Can you imagine this person as a father/mother to your children? Teaching them and nurturing them? Providing for you and them?

- Can you imagine going travelling with this person? Going on Umrah or Hajj together? Walking around the Kaabah together?

- How well do you think this person will fit into your family?

- Is being around them effortless?

- Do you want children? Do they?

- Are you someone who wants to live in an extended family? Are they? Or do they want to live independently? How do you feel about this? Is this something negotiable?

- What about going out to work? What are your expectations? Write these down. Discuss them with each other. Are you both career minded? Are you comfortable with both spouses working if they want to? If your spouse is very driven, are you willing to support them or will you resent them building their career and being out at work or locked away at home, focussing on work?

- Where do you want to live? How flexible about this are you both? Are you prepared to move away from family and friends? Relocate?

- What is your language of love? What is important to you? To your partner? Grand gestures? Gifts? Simplicity? Touch and intimacy? Spending time together?

- What are your expectations about how you spend your time?

- Is it to spend time just the two of you?

- Are you happy to be around lots of people,

- Do you prefer to spend time apart and alone as you pursue your own hobbies?

- How will you get the balance right when you are husband and wife?

- How important are your friends and family to each of you and how will you navigate existing relationships? What are your expectations around this? Talk this through.

- What are your expectations around things like:

  - Money: Are you a spender or a saver?

  - Food: Do you love to go out to eat or at home?

  - Sharing responsibilities: Do you see roles as traditional or are you flexible about these?

  - Spare time: Do you love to be doing things or are you a homebird?

  - Activities: Are you outdoorsy or is TV every night for you?

  - Timekeeping: Are you on time or chilled about this?

  - Planning: Are you a planner or spontaneous?

- Travel and holidays: Once a year or frequent flyer?

- Privacy: Are you selective about who you talk to or does everyone know your business?

Marrying a non-Muslim?

Whilst you may set out hoping to find a spouse, who not only shares your values but also your religious and cultural background, it is perfectly possible that you may find yourself drawn to someone from a different religion or no religion. If this happens, you may find yourself in a dilemma. Your family may have certain expectations of you, and you may struggle with how to navigate this. So what now?

The union of two people always needs compromise and adjustment. Marrying someone who does not share your faith is likely to bring additional challenges which it is worth thinking through before you make your decision. Food for thought below:

- Is my partner willing to become a Muslim? If not, then do I want to proceed with the marriage? Have this conversation early.

- If you do decide to proceed with marriage, think about the additional challenges that this will bring and how you will address them.

  - How will we bring up our children? As Muslim or not?

  - How do I/how does my partner feel about raising our children as Muslim or not?

  - Will the upbringing of our children be a struggle in the future? Will our children get confused if their parents follow different religions?

- What if you had aspirations of going on Hajj with your partner and they have decided not to become Muslim? How does this make you feel? Will you be happy going without them?

- Do you have dreams of praying side by side as a Muslim husband and wife? How will it make you feel to never fulfil this dream? Getting up for Fajr on your own?

- Think about your family traditions which are Islamic. How will you navigate these with a non-Muslim spouse?

- Are you on a spiritual journey? How would you feel about our spouse as you navigate the journey?

• If your partner does not become Muslim, and you decide to proceed with marriage and you decide to do Nikah, check that you can find someone who will agree to conduct the marriage ceremony for you. This can be a hurdle in some communities. It is worth doing the research early.

If it really matters to you that you are with a Muslim partner and you think that you will try and persuade your non-Muslim partner to change their religion once you are married, the questions below may be useful.

• Is it more respectful to your partner to have an open and honest conversation about what you really want now than to try and pressure them to change later?

• Ask yourself, what impact will this have on the marriage if I raise this after we are married?

- Assuming that you decide to go ahead and marry a partner from a different religion or cultural background, even if they become Muslim, have a think about and talk about any cultural differences which you may need to navigate. How will the families integrate/interact?

- How will I break it to my family? Be prepared for some difficult conversations and tense times, especially if they already have plans for you. Remember, always be respectful.

- Is there a supportive family member or friend who will help you speak with your parents?

- If your family is not in agreement, ask yourself, why this might be? Is this because your family wants the best for you?

- Is the objection from a place of concern and love?

- You may face a choice, your family or your partner? How does this make you feels? Imagine life without your family support? Or without your partner. It is a tough call.

- Is there someone in your circle who can guide you?

- Are you willing to make compromises?

- Most importantly, have you sought guidance from Allah? (see Istikhara)

Marrying an older woman

- What if there is a big age gap between me and my partner? Can I marry an older woman?

- What if she earns more money than me?

- What if she is my boss?

It is worth remembering that the Prophet's ﷺ first and most beloved wife was Bibi Khadija RA. She was 15 years his senior. She was the older woman. She was the Prophet's ﷺ boss. She was successful and wealthy and a respected businesswoman. This was a monogamous marriage, and the Prophet ﷺ was with his wife until she passed away. So, if you are in any doubt about marrying an older woman, a woman more successful than you or even your boss, the example of the Prophet ﷺ is a beautiful one.

Marrying more than one woman - Polygamy

It would be remiss not to mention polygamy and what to do if you are wondering about taking more than one wife or willing to be a co-wife. Think about what you want from your marriage. Do you have strong views about polygamy?

We won't go into specifics about polygamy here but remember that Nikah is a marriage contract. If you are planning on having a polygamous marriage as a man, or ladies, if you feel strongly that you will not tolerate being in a polygamous marriage, or you don't mind polygamy, then be totally clear, open and honest about this at the outset.

Talk it through with your partner before you get married and have the terms agreed in advance in your marriage contract. It is far less complicated to have an early conversation than to face polygamy later in the marriage and after children have been born.

Chapter Three: Now You're Engaged

Your engagement period is a crucial time for you to get to know each other's families. It is a good time to consider some of these questions.

- What are your family values? Do you have similar family values? Is this important to you?

- Do your families connect? How do you feel when you visit each other's families? Is there ease or discomfort?

- Do your parents get on with each other's parents and does this matter to you?

- Do you see yourself fitting into your spouse's family and vice versa?

- Does your future spouse get on with your parents or guardians and vice versa?

- How important is this to you?

- Are you planning on living in an extended family? If so then these questions may have a much greater significance.

- Can you imagine being able to live in an extended family with your future spouse? Does your future spouse fit into your family well enough to be able to live with them?

- As you spend more time together, it is worth thinking about how your future spouse makes you feel by how they react to things. Their reaction to things may reveal aspects of their character that you love or maybe not. Here are some example scenarios. Note how you feel if any of these or similar scenarios show up. What do the scenarios tell you about you and about your future spouse?

- How they react to the waitress in a restaurant who gets the order wrong.

- How they react to you being late/to them being late for an important meeting.

- Whether they treat people in general with respect.

- How they respond to you being forgetful.

- How they respond to members of their /your family.

- How they deal with a hard day at work – theirs and yours.

- How they respond to a last-minute emergency/change of plan.

- How you both respond to stressful situations and whether you are receptive to any suggestions that you each make to the other.

Ending an engagement that isn't working.

You may find that during your engagement period you learn things about yourself and your future spouse that make you unhappy and uncomfortable such that you decide to call it a day. Better now than after the Nikah and Alhamdulillah you still have the opportunity to gracefully bring things to a close. Always remember that it is your decision, and you must never feel that you must proceed with a marriage that you are unsure about.

Some dos and don'ts:

- Do end the engagement with dignity, grace and respect for the other person and their family.

- Do have any concluding conversation face to face and end the engagement with kind words.

- DO NOT end the engagement by text or WhatsApp!

Asking the parents/guardians

Do I need to ask my parents/guardians? These questions may help you to decide what to do.

- How will my parents/guardians feel if I don't seek permission?

- How loved and respected will they feel if I do?

- Whether I am required to or not, how much does it matter to me and my future spouse if I have their blessing? Or am I/ we indifferent to this?

- What impact will it have on my/our future relationship with them if I do not consult them and seek their blessing?

- And what about doing what is pleasing to Allah? How do I/we feel about this?

- Put yourself in the place of your parents/guardians and imagine how you would feel.

- If you decide not to ask permission, then think about how you will break the news to them and how this will play out.

Chapter Four: Preparing For The Big Day

Remember, the build up to the wedding day can be stressful. Kindness, consideration and patience will go a long way to help you navigate the build up to the big day and the day itself. Just a few things to think about!

- First things first: Set a date convenient to both families.

- Discuss and Decide

  - Venues, numbers of guests from each side and menus too.

  - Your budget – how much are you planning to spend?

  - Who is paying for the wedding? Will the families share the cost equally? Will it be paid for by the parents of bride? Will the bride and groom be paying for the wedding? It is good to get these things clarified.

  - Who you would each like to share your special day with you. Think about your wider family and friends and work together to make a list. Agree the list and invite away!

  - What will you be wearing? Will you want colour schemes?

  - Will you be hiring a wedding planner?

  - Will you have a traditional wedding?

- Does the venue have a licence to do a registry wedding as well as nikah or will you need two ceremonies?

Chapter Five: Making It Work

Navigating life together means talking about things, expressing your thoughts and expectations, being flexible and making compromises. Remember you are a couple who have decided to spend life together. It should be a joy to come home to each other. But you will come to crossroads and meet dark times. How you communicate with each other will be key.

Have a think about these!

- Practice daily gratitude for your partner and your marriage and appreciate the small things. Tell each other at least once a day how much you appreciate them.

- Practice forgiveness if things don't always go as planned. Let things go and avoid harbouring resentment. Talk to each other!

- Agree your boundaries and expectations but be fair and reasonable.

- Discuss the practical things such as :

    - Do you share chores or is there an expectation that one person will work and the other will look after the home? It is better to state your expectations than to sit quietly and expect the other person to be a mind reader or to build up resentment over time.

    - If one cooks does the other clean and vice versa?

    - The finances? Will you follow the Islamic model?

- Will you have a joint bank account? How will you manage this? If you are both working, is the expectation that you will put an equal amount into the account to run the household? Or are you planning on a different model? Talk about it and come to an agreement to avoid upsets later.

- What if you are living in an extended family? What are the expectations for each of you with behaviours, boundaries and finances? Be clear and avoid resentment build up.

- How will you communicate effectively? What if one you is working late and the other is waiting up for dinner?

- What about your pre-marriage friendships? What is the expectation there?

- How will you bring up your children?

- Whose family will you spend Ramadan/Eid with?

- How often are you comfortable with your spouse visiting his/her family?

- What about how you will spend your evenings and weekends/free time? What is your expectation?

Chapter Six: Sex and Intimacy in Marriage

Again, communication and compromise are key so make sure that you talk through your expectations of each other.

- Explore this together in a sensitive and loving way. Always remember that you are lovers. Remember to appreciate each other. Tell each other what you love about them. Make each other feel desired and wanted.

- What if I am attracted to someone outside of my marriage? How do I deal with that? Does it mean that I married the wrong person?

    - The guidance on this is simple. Be aware of your desire and head home. Seek love and passion and satisfaction from your spouse.

- Look at the examples of the Prophet ﷺ for guidance on this issue and so many questions that come up about this topic.

- What if the passion goes from our marriage? Be open with each other and talk about it. Don't be afraid to seek professional counselling and guidance.

Chapter Seven: Discussing Divorce

Remember that love takes effort. You need to work at loving each other and making each other feel loved. The act of loving someone is precious. So, if you feel that you no longer are in love or don't love your partner anymore then think about this carefully.

But if you have tried everything and you reach a place where your marriage has irretrievably broken down, then you may be thinking about parting company. This is as big a decision as when you got married, if not bigger, especially if you have children. Some questions to think about.

- What is making me so unhappy in this relationship that I am no longer prepared to stay and work things out?

- What good qualities do I see in my partner? Write down 10 qualities.

- Why did I choose my partner when I married them? Write down 10 reasons why.

- Now focus on these good qualities daily. Work on your own mindset and do some reframing.

- If you feel that your partner is being difficult, have you considered if they are OK?

- Have you thought about them and what they may be dealing with? Have you asked them?

- Have you tried talking to your spouse to identify and resolve the areas of unhappiness for you and for them?

- Have you considered going for marriage counselling? It may help to talk to someone independent.

- Have you thought about a mediator who is neutral and can work with you both?

- Have you tried taking some time apart to give each other a little breathing space?

- What about talking to your parents? Would this help?

- Have you considered the impact on your children? How will you feel about being a part time parent if you divorce?

- Have you thought about the practicalities of uncoupling? How will you navigate this?

- Have you sought guidance from Allah?

If you do decide that divorce is the only option for you both, then part with kindness, grace and dignity.